Applied Crime Analysis

Karim H. Vellani, CPO
and
Joel D. Nahoun

Butterworth–Heinemann
Boston   Oxford   Auckland   Johannesburg   Melbourne   New Delhi

Butterworth–Heinemann supports the efforts of American Forests and the Global ReLeaf program in its campaign for the betterment of trees, forests, and our environment.

Library of Congress Cataloging-in-Publication Data

Vellani, Karim H., 1971–
    Applied crime analysis / by Karim H. Vellani and Joel D. Nahoun.
        p.   cm.
    Includes bibliographical references and index.
    ISBN 0-7506-7295-1
    1. Crime analysis.   I. Nahoun, Joel D., 1971–   II. Title.
    HV7936.C88 V45   2000
    364'.042—dc21   00-41380

British Library Cataloguing-in-Publication Data
A catalogue record for this book is available from the British Library.

The publisher offers special discounts on bulk orders of this book.
For information, please contact:
Manager of Special Sales
Butterworth–Heinemann
225 Wildwood Avenue
Woburn, MA 01801-2041
Tel: 781-904-2500
Fax: 781-904-2620

For information on all Butterworth–Heinemann publications available,
contact our World Wide Web home page at: http://www.bh.com

10 9 8 7 6 5 4 3 2 1

Printed in the United States of America

Dedication

The authors would like to thank their fathers, Johnny Vellani and David Nahoun, without whose guidance, support, and compassion, this book would not have been possible. Thank you.

Epigraph

There is a strong family resemblance about misdeeds, and if you have all the details of a thousand at your finger ends, it is odd if you can't unravel the thousand and first.

... SIR ARTHUR CONAN DOYLE, A Study in Scarlet

Table of Contents

Introduction

THE CLIMATE

Little doubt changes in the past 25 years have reshaped the world, particularly, changes within both the domestic and international business worlds. The staggering transformation has truly awed everyone from captains of industry down to the casual observer. Whether one considers the meteoric rise of U.S. and international stock markets, the keen precision and blinding speed showcased in the latest technological breakthroughs, or the grandiose scale on which many businesses now operate, Americans have grown accustomed to the pursuit of excellence.

Indeed nothing quite captures the human imagination like an industry pioneer breaking the established mold and reaching beyond the goal into uncharted territory. Recent achievements in the sports world and the high-tech and Internet-related industries show that in all walks of life and manner of pursuits, everyone loves a winner. With this attachment to unsurpassed performance, however, has come a greater intolerance toward mediocrity or even perceived mediocrity. This almost phobic behavior pattern began gripping the American public during the mid-1980s when the nation sensed it was no longer alone as the world's financial, technological, and industrial leader. Some would cite the inevitability following the prosperous years of the early 1980s while others prophesied of permanent change in the manner business is conducted. This trend of ebb and flow continued through the next decade, and as the 1990s progressed, many companies that had enjoyed previous success began to struggle with domestic and international rivals, many producing comparable products at lower prices. In response, established companies began scaling down operations, or downsizing as it became known. In response, work environments operated at frenzied paces, and average workers were asked to leap higher for the purpose of clearing the raised bar of standards.

Global economic challenges continue to lay new foundations for the business world, and while the imagery may seem oppressive, the competitive spirit magnifies. Granted, raised standards, the cutthroat character of financial markets, and fierce competition produce both positive and negative effects. At its best, competition inspires one to attempt the unlikely and, at its worst, enables another to sink to common thievery. Thus, a delicate balance must be struck for the professional to be successful. Dedicated businesspeople must wear many hats simultaneously while keeping a watchful eye on the fiscal bottom line. The current workforce mandates a different worker than in decades past, one who merges diverse skills into low-risk, cost-efficient packages with a maximum potential upside, to use some contemporary business-speak.

Given the demands of average employers and strains placed on the workforce, it is not surprising or coincidental that the last 15 to 20 years have seen the growth of the how-to or do-it-yourself book genre. With employers expecting their workforce to be equipped with a cursory knowledge of most subjects and with the burden of attempting perfection causing the fault lines of sanity and emotional well-being to splinter, it is little wonder that help is needed and sought. This leads us to observe one major difference between this current generation of workers and those of decades past, which is, our predecessors often seemed reluctant to ask for help, while this generation appears at least willing to consider, if not embrace the notion.

THE PROBLEM

Environmental changes, both natural and manufactured, have affected our society, but perhaps the prevalence of crime, like terminal diseases, can cause the most influential lifestyle changes. So much is written and reported through print and electronic media about minor and catastrophic episodes of crime that often one finds oneself feeling immune or apathetic. Eventually, crimes tend to blend in with one another. This is not to propose that any one victimization is less or more significant than any other, but rather the sheer numbers in which they occur have shown the tendency to lure the populace into a state of anesthetization.

As businesspeople, crime awakens us from our stupor by interjecting itself into our interests and our personal lives, and that of our friends, relatives, and associates at vulnerable moments. It is only then that one realizes that the crime epidemic has struck. This of course happens outside the business realm as well, and again the realization is often a painful one, yet our awareness is certainly elevated. One has emerged from the anesthesia. For those engaged in property management, the line separating business and personal lives is often blurred, and the crime problem affecting one aspect generally threatens or imposes on the other. As conscientious businesspeople, one must remember that financial concerns aside, there is a human element to our decisions.

THE ACTION

Considering this dilemma, a property manager obviously has many issues with which to contend. Doubtless, the problem of crime, specifically how it relates to individual properties and surrounding areas, must be recognized and dealt with accordingly. This work was conceived to address the fundamental difficulties of contemporary business climates as they relate to the current crime situation. Singling out each problem and dealing with it individually would be too simple and unrealistic. A more holistic method would be to address the crime situation comprehensively while staying competitive, within budgetary restrictions, and not create prison-like facilities that may tend to scare off patrons. We hope we have accomplished this or at least planted the seeds of thought for those in property management to strike a balance between safety and freedom and thus fit the pieces of a difficult puzzle into place.

Purpose of Crime Analysis

When considering crime analysis, the most immediate images that occur to those not engaged in law enforcement, criminal justice, or the security industry can at times stray from the confines of reality and errantly veer toward fantasy. No doubt the term *crime analysis* is often confused with the act of solving a crime. This misnomer is in part due to incorrect emphasis of the various aspects of crime solving and crime prevention in popular culture. At times such famous fictional detectives as Sir Arthur Conan Doyle's Sherlock Holmes, Agatha Christie's Hercule Poirot and Miss Marple characters, as well as those creations of writers of contemporary police procedure mysteries, including television's Colombo, are credited for what is commonly believed to be the only form of crime analysis. In actuality, these fictional sleuths are practicing traditional criminology, which is the scientific deduction and investigation of crime with emphasis on who committed the crime and why the crime was committed, leading to the end purpose of apprehending the criminal and bringing closure to the criminal case. While from a semantical standpoint these detectives did engage in the analysis of crime, for property management purposes, crime analysis has a very different meaning.

If traditional criminology is the re-enactment of a crime for purposes of bringing it to closure, then crime analysis is the autopsy that will provide solutions to the security breach that enabled the commission of the offense in order to enhance crime prediction capabilities and to develop proactive approaches to security and prevention. In broad terms, crime analysis is the logical examination of crimes that have penetrated preventive measures. Included in the examination are the frequency of specific crimes, each incident's temporal details (time and day), and the risk posed to a property's inhabitants, as well as the application of revised security standards and preventive measures that, if adhered to and monitored, can be the panacea for a given crime dilemma. This practice, while being disciplined work, is not glamorous. However, for its sublime purpose of working to reduce crime at a particular site, it is as effective as the deductive reasoning used by master criminologists found in film and literature. In a sense, the two disciplines, Criminology and Crime Analysis, are similar, as both tend to carefully collect and examine facts about crime and use logical reasoning to reach their respective conclusions.

It is not without purpose that the scientific study of criminal perpetrators has been referred to as traditional criminology. Recent criminological theory has changed focus from an offender-based to a target-oriented foundation, a shift designed toward blocking criminal opportunities at the property level. This innovative concept is not meant as a replacement for traditional criminology, but as an alternative, yet complementary ideology bringing together property managers, security professionals, public law enforcement, citizens, and the common goal of crime prevention. Traditional criminology will remain and continue to contemplate the conventional issues in criminal justice, with primary consideration for offenders and their apprehension. However, conventional criminology's deficiency in explaining why some places are more crime prone than others and how crime is patterned both temporally and spatially is the prerequisite for advancement (Maguire, Morgan, and Reiner, 1997). Thus, this new target-specific philosophy, rooted in the theories of Rational Choice, Routine Activity, Situational Crime Prevention, and Crime Pattern, has been dubbed alternative criminology, or for brevity's sake, alt-criminology. Where alt-criminology's forefathers laid the theoretical groundwork, this text follows with its practical application, crime prevention through analysis.

With a working definition of crime analysis, one can recognize when and how to use it. To better understand how crime analysis can be approached (after all, it is often difficult to imagine a course of action without first surveying the scenario and thus becoming aware of the overall objective), let us create a hypothetical management situation in which crime analysis is not considered or not a known option prior to prescribing crime prevention measures.

APPLICATION: FICTIONAL SCENARIO

For our scenario, the reader should place himself in the role of a property manager of an office building located in the midst of a metropolitan business district. Every nook and cranny from the suites contained within, the lobby, the hallways, and all common areas are under our manager's control, including the attached parking garage. Aspects that our manager is concerned with range from rudimentary building safety (i.e., assurances that the foundation will not suddenly give way or that the roof will not collapse, as well as assurances that the building falls within the city or county fire code) to potential safety hazards in the common areas (slippery surfaces and the like) to overall safety and the sense of well-being in the relatively isolated atmosphere of the parking garage. One should remember that management fees are correlational to the quality delivered in overseeing the building and its tenants' general well-being. After all, income generated through the tenants maintains the building's financial stability.

Having created this fictional scenario, let us eliminate from the equation the unaccountable element of chance that our manager's property over others in the area is singled out and is most frequently victimized. To be judicious, one must consider that because our property is located in a high-traffic atmosphere and also where the average employee's annual salary falls between $35,000 and $40,000, one should expect that the employees in the building and their automobiles may be considered ripe targets for crime tribulations.

Our manager's tenure began five years ago, and at present, he is in the process of self-evaluation. Overall, there is some good news to report. Building occupancy is at 85 percent, which he could improve upon, but on the whole, the property has been a success. As this period of reckoning is known to all parties concerned throughout the building, a committee representing the tenants has presented a list of grievances. It soon becomes quite clear that the manager's perception of building maintenance and security is markedly different from that of the building tenants. This is not to say that our manager is completely ignorant of problem areas, but according to the tenants, his knowledge of criminal incidents is not complete. As such, our manager must address the tenants' concerns with due diligence. In most cases, the tenants are satisfied with their lease agreements' general provisions; rent is reasonable, with the prime location justifying the expense. Structural safety is not an issue as the building is well made and new enough not to have degenerated in appearance or integrity. The tenant's chief concern is crime on the property, primarily in the parking garage, and its direct effect on the building employees. Certainly crime reports have filtered in, but surely not at the alarming frequency that the committee reports. Our manager has been operating under the assumption that he knew about all criminal activity occurring on his property. As proof of the crime situation, the committee spokesperson presented the manager with a table of the property's criminal activity during the past five years:

Table 1–1 Five-Year Crime Listing.

Auto Theft	197
Theft (from offices, cars, and common areas)	432
Robbery	19
Burglary (of offices)	47
Aggravated Assault	27
Rape	3
Murder	1

Our manager is shocked to learn the magnitude of criminal activity that has taken place and escaped his watchful eye. Perhaps the overall financial success of the building has lulled him into wrongly believing the extent of his effectiveness. Beyond the grievances, his attorney and accountant prepared a confidential outline of the potential consequences of crime on the property:

1. High employee turnover for most tenants is partially attributable to crime in the parking garage and other common areas.
2. Many complaints to tenants from their customers regarding the lack of building security.
3. Six discontinuations of leases at the time of renewal, due to the crime situation.
4. A lawsuit has been filed against the building's owners and our fictitious manager alleging failures to provide adequate security.
5. Possible punitive reparations from the pending lawsuit should the jury find in the plaintiff's favor.
6. Time, effort, and money spent in mounting a defense against litigation.
7. Noticeable decrease in occupancy rates (from 95 percent to 85 percent) and associated revenue attributable to tenant pullouts during the past year.
8. Tarnished reputation as property manager and management company.
9. Potential increases in insurance rates if the company is found negligent in the pending lawsuit.

Our manager's accountant and attorney have conveyed grave financial consequences that will develop should present conditions perpetuate, giving our manager convincing evidence to act quickly and appropriately to reduce potential damage. He is at fault for not paying requisite attention to the specific and general details regarding security interests. Mistakes must be admitted and corrected. After some thought, he maps out three avenues to take:

1. Inactivity. Simply hoping that the crime problem will go away and leave the building and profit margins intact. As an

experienced manager, he realizes that this path will lead to his management company's demise. After being apprised of the actual crime level on the property and the associated costs, the manager is even more aware that profits are not mutually exclusive of management responsibilities.

2. Reactivity. In his building's current state, this would entail the immediate hiring of security personnel and application of upgraded security measures for a limited, temporary time as budget permits. He weighs this move carefully for several reasons: (1) it is his usual course of action; (2) he knows it well, and it provides a level of comfort; (3) this is the road that led to his current position; (4) it is costly; (5) this course will not likely appease the tenants this time. As his logic progresses, he feels that reactivity, if not successful over the long term, will not grant him the opportunity to begin anew with the tenants and may ruin this business relationship with the building's owners. Though reactivity was ruled out, he did consider this move more carefully than the first. He is on the right track.

3. Proactivity. Between the previous two options lies a third, which is to learn more about the crime picture and its causation factors using crime analysis. Armed with the right information and techniques, he can work to eradicate crime on the property holistically, by first understanding the origins of the problem, its enabling factors, and the preventive measures necessary to minimize, if not eliminate, emerging crime scenarios. This idea is appealing in that he is working to solve the base problem rather than the symptoms, and it allows him to easily justify security expenditures to appease the building's owners.

Of the three options, the third makes the most sense as it is the most prudent and in the long term will be the most cost-effective of his choices. Counseling with the business-oriented side of his brain, he knows learning more and acting on an empirical base will serve to protect his interests from the consequences of crime. In selecting this third option, he sets aside the immediate problems and determines that it would be best to become armed with actual knowledge and the empowerment needed to negate the existing dilemmas and render them harmless.

As the journey through crime analysis continues, the reader should keep the fictional scenario in mind, as it will be referenced frequently. In subsequent chapters, the crime analysis methodology will be discussed in greater detail, but for now a more intuitive overview of what crime analysis is, what it accomplishes, and how it works should be considered. Following is a list of the many aspects of crime analysis and the goals it attempts to achieve:

1. To reduce crime on the property.
2. To evaluate and aid in the selection of security and crime prevention measures.
3. To justify security and crime prevention expenditures.
4. To provide a system of monitoring the effectiveness of security and crime prevention measures.
5. To provide a continual evaluation system of the property's crime situation.
6. To reduce the liability of property owners and their agents (property managers and security companies).

Regarding the broader objectives and benefits crime analysis aspires to and if properly used, generally provides, one must be cognizant that the most notable and tangible goals are the saving of time and money, which in many businesses are one in the same. Of course, updating and correcting previously faulty and ineffective security measures can save a property manager money, and prevention can cut down on liability, which can be measured in reparation of damages for loss and injury. What must also be considered is the time it takes to handle such matters. Yet crime analysis helps in other financial concerns as careful thought and more information and the subsequent flexibility among options almost always positively affects the bottom line and increases the probability of success.

Many would recognize the dangers of reactivity. Think about how the great financiers of our time have had the vision to discern trends while those that history has forgotten remained static, cutting their losses. Most would rather strive to be more like an Andrew Carnegie or John D. Rockefeller than those whom history has seen fit to exclude based on their mediocrity. Think of proactivity as foresight and reactivity as procrastination.

CRIME ANALYSIS CHARACTERISTICS

Crime analysis is a detail-oriented discipline wherein the analyst endeavors to seek the truth of a given situation utilizing methods and the right information to confirm the truth so that an effective plan can be formulated. With that path laid forth, prevention components are set in motion to accomplish the intermediate goals of the plan, which together comprise a winning strategy over crime. This must sound very impressive, but one intangible of crime analysis is empowerment and the peace of mind that cannot be measured in dollars and cents. Having seen some of the more obvious goals and plateaus one can reach utilizing crime analysis to control the consequences of crime on property, due consideration is given to the reasons that make it work and in effect, support the concept.

First, the level of accuracy crime analysis provides in relation to diagnosing a crime problem is superior to that of making an uninformed, perceptually incorrect judgment. What must first be observed are the problem itself, the type of crime, when it was committed, and the location of the crime on the property. Beyond surface level, crime analysis reveals more subtle crime differences that will help in the selection of crime countermeasures. Was vandalism of a vehicle simply vandalism, or was it an attempt to steal the vehicle? Was an assault actually an attempted rape?

Another aspect of accuracy is the source of a crime, exactly how it became an issue on the property, and prescribing the most suitable solution. From this point, crime patterns and trends will emerge and lead to a solution or, at the very least, provide guidance on ruling out ineffectual courses of action. The difficulty in maintaining accuracy depends on the complexity of the problem. Depending on the scope of an investigation, crime analysis can utilize the nth degree as criminal incidents are treated as element-specific as possible to diagnose and prescribe an appropriate solution for a given crime problem. Solid crime analysis avoids the pitfalls of considering incidents in the offender-specific sense, which is the task of criminal justice practitioners, not those involved in security and crime prevention. This type of crime analysis is a separate discipline and usually falls under the jurisdiction of public sector law enforcement, the court system, and prisons.

While the crime analysis discussed in subsequent chapters concentrates on singular properties, it is commonplace that the efforts of one conscientious property manager work to spark interest in addressing the security concerns of other properties. Those crime deterrents found on one site may discourage crime in the general area—diffusion of benefits. Crime prevention can also increase crime in the area—crime displacement (see Chapter 5 for a discussion of Crime Displacement and Diffusion of Benefits).

Be it superficial reasoning that a criminal is met with adequate preventive measures and decides that the area may not be suitable for the criminal task at hand and leaves, the job of prevention has been accomplished and additional benefits have come to fruition. This aspect is especially intriguing with the recent arrival of community policing, which is a philosophy directed toward crime not as dependent on public law enforcement as past conventional wisdom dictated. By no means does this ideal embrace the brand of vigilante justice featured in the films of Charles Bronson, Chuck Norris, or Steven Seagal, but rather it aims to realize that public law enforcement cannot be everywhere. A measure of accountability by community members, including businesses and residents, can compensate with neighborhood watches, partnerships for safe areas, and in general, a cognizant eye toward environmental changes, which alleviate crime pressures.

Among other notions found when a more discriminative approach is applied is the diagnosis of a specific crime problem at a specific site. Through research and record-keeping of crimes and categorization by type of offense, location, time, and so forth, patterns and trends will emerge, and like medical doctors equipped with fact, an educated judgment can be made about what the problem is and to what extent the property is affected. Only then can the proper treatment be administered.

Where do a property manager's responsibilities lie? Crime analysis helps to differentiate between a property manager's area of control (Circle of Control) and the areas over which managers have influence (Circle of Influence). (See Figure 1–1.) By circle of control, the property manager limits his concern to only that physical area that he is charged to oversee. In contrast, the circle of influence includes areas outside immediate control. Using the building manager scenario as an example, our manager is responsible for the

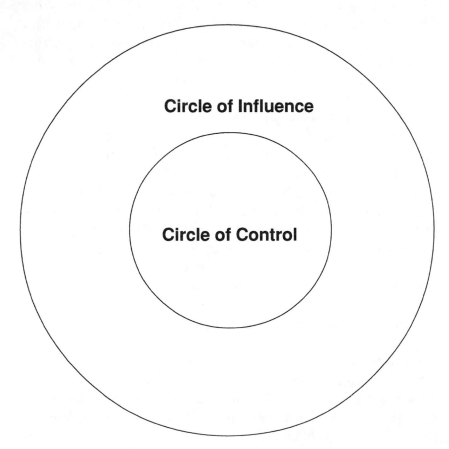

Figure 1–1.   Circle Of Control/Influence

building's operation, the common areas, and the parking garage, which constitute his circle of control. An example of an area within his Circle of Influence is the property next door, a strip center used daily by his tenants. The proximity of this strip center to his building, its use by his tenants, and his relationship with that center's management place this facility within his Circle of Influence. Though he is not responsible for this facility, it does affect his property's security and vice-versa.

As facts accumulate and problems are diagnosed, crime analysis aids in planning crime prevention and improving the probability of success. There is no short-term slide rule that can measure how much prevention is enough or too much; that will come with experience, from research of other similar situations, and through the advice of security and crime prevention experts. Nevertheless, the first step is the consideration of actual threats and the selection of a plan that defines resources correlational to asset values, the extent of possible losses, and the probability of that loss, basically a cost-benefit analysis. What seems hopelessly complex right now will appeal more to common sense, through the absorption of crime analysis techniques, and the individual property manager's understanding and overall knowledge of his property.

Lastly, one will find that crime analysis does not stop at diagnosis and application of a crime prevention program, but takes further steps to monitor the crime picture continually after resources have been deployed and plans put into action. In a sense, it presents a set of checks and balances that can provide warning signs if the criminal element is catching up to preventive measures and allows room for redesign and revision if the nature of crime on the property changes, subsides, or advances. One clear staple of crime analysis is that it is dynamic in nature, provides for change, and will not commit the property manager to a singular course of action. In many ways learning crime analysis is like learning to think like a chess player, that is, considering every available move, allowing logic and reason to support candidate moves, finalizing a move based on further thought, and still leaving room for maneuverability with the changing times.

2

Uses of Crime Analysis

Perhaps the most fundamental of concepts regarding human existence and relations with others is identity; indeed it is present in all aspects of life. It can be argued that every time one begins anew in any scenario, be it a job promotion, a career change, a business partnership, marriage, or parenthood, identity must be addressed.

As with other new beginnings, identity is as appropriate a place as any to embark on a journey through crime analysis. In defining the various practitioners of crime analysis, one can hope to foster a greater understanding of one's own presence in the realm, which crime analysis, crime prevention, management, and operations co-inhabit. Identity asks the "who" question in the manner that a newspaper reporter gathers and correlates facts for a news story. Who are the practitioners of crime analysis and what abilities set them apart from those not utilizing or only considering crime analysis? To be perfectly candid, very little separates those who practice crime analysis from those who do not. Truly, crime analysis is one of the few disciplines that works to attain measurable ends while not requiring extensive cross-scholarship to other disciplines. What is required, though, is a willingness to allow reason to rule absolute, and the capacity to juxtapose collected crime data and practical crime prevention application, concepts firmly rooted in the progressive doctrine of alt-criminology.

Essentially, two categories of crime analysis practitioners can be discerned: First, property managers and property owners, who share similar interests, though differences do exist; and second, the security services provider, who is contracted by a property's administrator to meet the crime analysis and prevention task on behalf of management. The group of practitioners composed of property owners and property managers are found to operate so closely, often synonymously, that overlap is consistent enough that it becomes cumbersome to make distinctions between the two. Thus, unless a marked difference persists, owners and managers will represent one in the same and be denoted by manager.

PROPERTY MANAGERS DEFINED

Generally speaking, property managers are those people who own or are contractually obligated to manage a property that is open to the public or where members of the citizenry are otherwise invited. These managers operationally control such places as schools, shopping malls, strip centers, gas stations, hotels, motels, office buildings, parking structures, convenience stores, retail stores, residential buildings and complexes, banks, stadiums and arenas, and other similar entities. The people who use these properties for legitimate reasons and are, in essence, the property's financial bloodline, are referred to as consumers. Consumers predominantly have limited ability and choice to reduce, deter, or prevent crime on another's property and tend to rely on crime prevention measures of which they are aware. As will be discovered, property managers may be legally required to provide reasonable security if certain precursor factors exist. Some experts have suggested that property managers have a moral obligation to take the necessary steps to reduce crime and protect their consumers (Souryal, 1998).

One can literally select any company and detail a different hierarchy structure and, within that, a chain of command affecting the ability to carry out the crime analysis task and supplemental improvements to their current crime prevention system. To varying degrees, all property managers are concerned with their crime prevention plan's effectiveness, as well as the impact of the surrounding area's criminal activity on their property. More importantly though, they are interested in minimizing the cost of conducting efficient operations to achieve crime prevention ends. A hands-on property manager held accountable for a single property may not have access to all the resources that are normally available to property managers in a large property management company. Thus, distinctions between property managers can be drawn, based on their property's type and geographic area, the resources available, and the civil liability to which they may be susceptible. Each of these factors will be examined with their effects on management's ability to carry out crime analysis and prevention.

Despite potential differences, at least one similarity, a common thread so to speak, is discernable from the crime analysis vantagepoint; that is, ultimately property managers must place emphasis on the individual property when planning and working to prevent crime. One may be inclined to wonder why this is. The answer, as discovered from alt-criminology (see Chapters 4 and 5), is that property managers infrequently experience crimes at all their properties by the same criminal perpetrator. Criminals generally do not select targets simply because they are owned or managed by a certain company, and more often, are oblivious to company divisions. This suggests that management, in striving to increase profit and reduce liability, should allocate resources based on an individual property's needs, rather than an equal distribution among properties. With the circles of influence and control in mind, one should begin to understand the importance of property-specific (target-oriented) crime analysis and prevention and the factors that influence its implementation.

GROWTH OF PREMISES SECURITY

Premises security has become a growth industry in which lawyers and expert witnesses have made solid reputations and considerable fortunes. Rapidly evolving in the court system rather than through legislative acts, it is cumbersome, yet vital to keep abreast of changes in legal decisions and standards. Laws, in general, are peculiar and while in some cases make perfect sense, their absence of application and enforcement in other cases render them somewhat unreliable. A fortunate characteristic of crime analysis is that it is open to everyone and not solely intended for those who are required to do so or those engaged in the legal or security professions. The information necessary to conduct crime analysis is available and remains above the red tape of typical bureaucratic channels.

Premises Security Defined

A premises security lawsuit is a civil action brought on behalf of a person seeking damages for negligent security against the owners and their agents (management and security companies) of the property where the injury or loss occurred. Generally, three elements must be met in order for a plaintiff to prevail in a premises security lawsuit. These elements are duty, breach of duty, and proximate cause. These issues are considered in depth in Chapter 9. For now, some facts that lead to the seriousness of this issue should be uncovered.

STATISTICS

A study of 1992 lawsuits conducted by the U.S. Department of Justice revealed that juries found in favor of the plaintiff more than 50 percent of the time, awarding an estimated $2.7 billion in damages. Almost 10 percent of the jury awards were for more than $1,000,000 (DeFrances, Smith, and Langan, 1995). Similarly, a private sector analysis found that almost 30 percent of the cases were in favor of the plaintiff or settled with an average jury award/settlement of $1.2 million (Blake and Bradley, 1999). This study also indicated that the average settlement reported in these types of cases was over $500,000 (Kaminsky, 1995). In breaking down the crimes leading up to the lawsuits, assault and battery accounted for 39.5 percent of the cases, rape and sexual assault, 27 percent; robbery, 10.3 percent; and wrongful death, 15.4 percent (Blake and Bradley, 1999).

General

As revealed by the jury award and settlement statistics, negligent security can be catastrophic to a business. The problem is more than a win-lose situation; even when the property manager prevails, litigation costs can be extreme, up to and exceeding $50,000. Beyond financial devastation, litigation may also mean lost productivity; high turnover of employees, customers, and tenants; low morale; and poor public relations, not to mention the stress of being involved in a lawsuit.

Prevention Costs

What is now evident is that crime prevention is significantly less costly to property management than a settlement, and especially less costly than a defeat in court. "The cost of potential litigation prevention is one of the intangible balancing factors between income and expenses" (Blake and Bradley, 1999). Potential liability situations can be avoided if management responds appropriately to their property's crime experience. Premises security cases are much less supportable if management conducts crime analysis, anticipates certain activity, and implements reasonable crime countermeasures.

A central, yet often overlooked, issue for property managers implementing crime prevention is the type of property under their care. Generally, some properties are more attractive to the criminal element than others, and more precisely, particular properties may attract specific categories of crime. Through use of crime analysis, the crime category can be identified and anticipated, thus indicating the crime prevention measures to be employed on that specific property. Specific property concerns are explored in Chapter 8.

Property managers, like all good businesspeople, usually know the characteristics of their consumers (customers, guests, tenants, etc.). Similarly, they have an educated opinion of why consumers choose their property over similar properties to shop, live, and visit. In this same fashion, property managers need to understand the unique characteristics of the land and structures under their super- vision, specifically the land boundaries, traffic levels, common areas, parking facilities, and areas not open to the public, such as private offices, storage areas, janitorial stations, and utility rooms. A thor- ough understanding of the property's capacity to attract crime will help management develop a complete crime prevention program.

Perhaps the most significant effect of company structure in regards to crime analysis is budgeting for such operations. Budget, more so than other business-related matters, cannot be ignored. Quite simply understood, the nature of all those who either labor just to survive or those who thrive with higher levels of success will not allow budget to be forgotten. Thus, crime analysis can be both restricted and empowered by the business budget. Surely financial resources can play an important role in creating an extensive crime prevention program geared for longevity and effectiveness, but money alone is not the crime prevention solution, and money alone cannot compensate for lacking knowledge of crime analysis. Again, harkening back to the company structure, budgets will differ pro- portionately to the size of the company, the innate cost to run the business in which the company is engaged, and of course, the effi- ciency of the operations, including the fluidity of funds allotted to cover crime prevention programs.

Of course, the possibility exists that a company in need of revamped property crime prevention may operate under the premise that an expert in the field will perform at a higher level than one from their own ranks. The company, therefore, delegates that job to one specializing in that particular field, so as not to detract from that company's actual business, which defines its very existence and maintains the livelihood of everyone involved. Budget considerably affects the control given to independent agencies to which crime pre- vention aspects are sometimes outsourced. This group is usually a security services provider. Typically, these providers are called on to handle aspects of physical security such as security personnel, sur- veillance cameras (CCTV), access control systems, and sometimes the drafting of policies and procedures to reinforce the more tangible measures. Much of the work undertaken by security services providers is clearly circumscribed by property management from the beginning. Property managers retaining security services often adhere to general visions of what the circumstances are relative to a given property's perceived crime and have an approximate idea of what needs to be accomplished to control or eradicate an existing crime problem. Metaphorically, this is similar to enlisting a mechanic to fix a car's problem, which may not be evident to the untrained eye. And even if the problem is known, a specific set of skills and resources are often needed to actually confront the task at hand and see its completion despite budgetary and time constraints. Professional security companies should strive to attain as much free reign as possible over matters they are charged to handle. Not only do they have the job to protect as independent security professionals, but also they are held in higher regard than others securing the property. Certainly effective crime analysis can enhance a security company's service by pinpointing areas of weakness in a client's property and across a number of properties. For security service providers, crime analysis operates as a tool to increase sales to future clients, as well as maximizing potential with existing customers. In this sense, utilizing crime analysis can help a security company stand out from the crowd of other security service providers.

APPLICATION: FICTIONAL SCENARIO

In Chapter 1, our fictional property manager was faced with an existing crime problem on his property. His options were to stand pat and ignore the problem, implement gross measures on a temporary basis, or become personally involved in security and crime prevention. Within that scenario exists the two main categories of crime analysis practitioners and also the subcategory of independent owner, as our manager is also the building owner.

What has been discussed in this chapter will be applied using the scenario. Though our protagonist is sole owner, he cannot make the erroneous assumption that his decisions affect only his interests or that these interests are exclusive to business aspects measurable solely by profit and loss statements. His decisions involve the personal safety, well-being, and peace of mind for all of the property's consumers.

Our hypothetical manager owns and manages the office building and the parking garage. Those are his direct responsibilities. However, there are indirect areas of responsibility, where if a crime were to transpire, he could be held accountable, such as walkways that border his office space and areas where public telephones are accessible. These are within his circle of control. Within his circle of influence are neighboring open spaces, vacant buildings, and high-traffic streets that may also pose risks that contain potential danger that can threaten to spill over onto his property and create a hazardous situation. (See Figure 2–1.)

It should be understood that the criminal element is not denoted by the moniker underworld without reason, and where there is ignorance of the threat, there is a potential for illegal activity and civil liability. As learned earlier, our manager was preparing to face the aggravation of a lawsuit claiming inadequate security, for which he will lose time, spend money, and develop additional stress regardless of the lawsuit's outcome. One must understand, however, that the purpose of law is not to interfere with the life of a particular business as long as the premise of that business resides within the law, but rather the law is a benefit to society as a whole.

With that understanding, an aloof manager may choose not to spare the time devising security policies or to ask the occasional probing question. An aloof manager will fail to seize the initiative of learning the property's innate criminal nature, much less spend money on hard security measures or hiring security personnel to patrol the grounds. An astute businessperson, however, realizes that the fruit of finely honed management skills is a comfortable and profitable working relationship with both customers and employees. Thousands of managers, perhaps paying attention to the ideas mentioned above, especially where they apply to crime and liability reduction, can save millions of dollars.

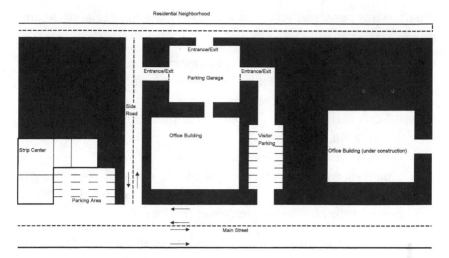

Figure 2–1. Property Diagram

Delving further into application, our manager, having decided to become a more conscientious administrator, has taken to stalking the property night and day, clipboard in hand, to detail the areas he is responsible for and what other factors affect his property's welfare. Most immediate and recognizable are the main entrance, side entrances, individual suites, common areas, walkways to the building from the garage, walkways leading to access streets, and of course, the parking garage. Within this list, there are many more nuances to observe and that deserve his undivided attention. This exercise of creating a checklist serves two purposes. It delineates points of concern to be addressed, and it orientates the mind toward troubleshooting.

Main Entrance

The main entrance is of particular importance because of its proximity to the parking garage and the high pedestrian traffic, as most or all people entering the building will pass through this point. Our manager enters this area and notes concerns for consideration as befits his responsibility. He asks himself some of the questions pertinent to this particular area, but that can be asked in relation to any property.

1. Generally speaking, is the main entrance a secure area?
2. Is access open to anyone who wishes to enter?
3. Is that access monitored?
4. What measures exist to bar unauthorized personnel from utilizing the entrance?
5. What is the visibility level at this area?
6. Can responsible parties see out of the entrance and to what extent? Is the range of vision such that the whole parking garage walkway can be seen from the inside?

Our manager looks down at his list, and while pleased, is astounded at the level of thinking he has reached in merely scrutinizing the main entrance. Outside, our manager heads to a primary area of his property's crime, the above-ground parking garage.

Side Entrance

1. Who has access to the side entrance?
2. Do employees and tenants use the side entrance as a primary entrance?
3. Will the closing off of this entrance allow easier monitoring of who is entering the premises through the main entrance?

Parking Garage

1. Is the walkway between the parking garage and building protected by any barriers that would prevent an offender from approaching? Conversely, are there barriers that mask the walkway from view in such a way that an attacker can carry out a crime without detection from the people in the building or other public view?
2. In transition from the walkway to the parking garage, is there ample light to see where one is going?
3. Entering the parking garage, are there spaces where criminals may hide, and can that space be amply lit or blocked from entry?

4. Do the elevators connecting to other parking levels work properly? Do they open to remote parts of the garage? Are these areas amply lit, and do they harbor open spaces where attackers may conceal themselves?
5. Is the parking garage regularly policed for security breaches or unauthorized personnel? Do security officers patrol the area? In vehicles or on foot?
6. Is an access control system in place to prevent unauthorized persons from entering the parking garage?
7. Do security policies provide for the meaningful reporting of incidents?
8. Is there any way for potential victims to call for assistance? Are panic buttons installed?
9. Does policy allow for escorts to or from the parking garage and vehicles if requested?
10. Are staircases connecting levels of the parking garage secured (lighting, hiding places, other safety precautions)? Are the steps remotely located?
11. Are users of the parking garage required to have identification badges on vehicles or some other access pass?
12. Are parking spaces clearly denoted for employees, and visitors?
13. Is there a distinct flow of traffic within the parking garage, and is it easily discernable?
14. Are there blind spots when the parking garage opens up to main or side streets?

Next our manager enters the building and inspects the common areas, which would include interior elevators, washrooms, conference rooms, and hallways.

Common Areas
1. In general, are there places where unauthorized personnel may hide?
2. Are the common areas visible from the lobby/main entrance or comparable vantagepoint?

General

1. Is there a quick and efficient means to report injury, attacks, or concerns to management or security personnel?
2. Are conference rooms locked and restricted to authorized personnel?
3. Are utility closets and electrical rooms kept locked and off limits to all but authorized staff?

Individual Suites

1. Are suites secured?
2. Is a system in place to report incidents directly to management?
3. Are walkways connecting suites to elevators and stairs free of hiding places?
4. Are inside walkways monitored via CCTV or other means?
5. Can a CCTV system be installed if crime analysis dictates?
6. Are there windows, and if so, are they free of signage to assist in visibility from offices?
7. Does management maintain a list and photograph of each employee, including what areas they are authorized to access? Would this be feasible?

Old Management vs. New Management

Our conscientious manager realizes that these are the areas and details within his circle of control with which he must be concerned. Considering this responsibility, the myth of the building manager sitting behind a desk in some remote location only coming on property to collect rent is quickly dispelled. Of course, a myth is not without some basis in fact, and hundreds if not thousands of managers have existed by doing just that; but as times change, their ways will prove to be outdated, and the future's landscape has no place for outmoded and stagnant thinking. Having swept through his building, our manager admits to himself the true magnitude of his obligation. Properly warmed to the task and indeed inspired, he adds another section to his areas of concern.

Surrounding Areas

These areas consist of areas bordering his properties on all four sides. While these are territories that belong to other managers and in some cases the municipality, they are in his circle of influence and enter into his holistic examination of property security and ultimately, crime prevention. These areas comprise:

 ◆ North, behind the parking garage, a residential neighborhood.
 ◆ Southward, the main thoroughfare.
 ◆ To the West, across the side street, the strip center used by the building's tenants and the general public.
 ◆ And finally, a half-constructed building to the East.

In relation to this, his circle of influence, our manager notes further considerations:

1. In the adjacent residential neighborhood, what is the level of crime?
2. To what extent does that crime level impact his property?
3. Do these areas provide hiding places or escape routes for attackers?
4. What can be done to prevent criminal activity from stemming from that area?
5. Are those employees who depend on public transportation safe from criminal elements while traversing between bus stops and the building?
6. Are the bushes and trees trimmed sufficiently to not create visibility problems or concealment issues?

Beyond these areas lies the municipality at large and the myriad concerns it brings. To examine how the manager can best assess the threat of criminal activity posed to the property, the sources of crime data and statistics, which are imperative to any crime analysis, will be discussed, as well as the various levels that analysis can aspire to given its intended scope.

3

Data Sources

Within every endeavor into the arts and sciences, lies a basis from which one can expand and build outward. Painters have their canvases, physicists have models of cells and atoms, chemists have solutions, and crime analysts have their statistics. It is from these statistics and data sets that the analyst synthesizes figures into natural language characterizations of crime frequencies and rates on the property, in the area, and in relation to much larger areas.

Crime data is intriguing in that it attempts to provide an accurate picture of criminal activity at a particular location. Statistics represent criminal activity in the form of numbers, comparable to an inventory, in which the crime analysis task is the reformation of that activity as a tangible tool for risk management. Like a baseball scorecard that records the game's details chronologically, crime analysis converts its source data into a reconstruction of what transpired on the property. One can think of data sets as a zipped computer file made up of raw data, with the crime analyst acting as the extraction tool. Of course, crime analysis is much more than simple extraction. It is the ability to discern one data set's source from another to find which is applicable to cogent analysis. But, this skill cannot be mastered without knowledge of the different data types, from where they originate, and what potential they hold in terms of the end result. The data sets and associated sources examined include demographic data, the Federal Bureau of Investigation's Uniform Crime Reports, local police records including Calls for Service and Offense Reports, and security records maintained by property management and their agents.

CALLS FOR SERVICE (CFS)

The primary data set is Calls for Service (CFS), which serves as crime analysis' basis and provides for the most accurate portrayal of criminal and other activity at a property. One can think of CFS as the complete array of fragments that, when joined, form the most strikingly grounded survey of criminal activity for a specific property. CFS consist of every report of crime, suspected crime, and activity called in to the police from a property. No other crime information source is as focused on a specific address for such a vast time span as CFS, with the possible exception of in-house security reports generated by personnel operating on property 24 hours a day, 7 days a week. These inclusions, by definition, omit the imprecise factor of unreported crime. Research has concluded that unreported crime accounts for a 10 percent higher crime index, though this is highly dependent on the type of crime under observation. Despite the exclusion of unreported crime, CFS still provide representative illustrations of criminal activity on a property.

CFS are those crimes or other activity reported by a victim, witness, or other person to a local law enforcement agency via the 911 emergency system and other channels. These reports may consist of actual crimes, from murder to theft, or suspicious activity, and other incidents such as missing children, motor vehicle accidents, and parking complaints. Whatever the concern, if it is reported by a person, it is noted by the law enforcement agency. The synopsis of the given incidents is included on the record along with the location, date, and time the event was reported. From devastatingly influential to seemingly insignificant, these records exist as clues waiting to be examined in some Holmesian mystery. Because of their completeness of representation and maintenance by a local governing body, and because they operate independent from the property manager's interests, they can generally be considered objective, thus adding the first of many threads of reliability to the crime analysis conclusions. In addition to the more obvious crimes, CFS add elements that may be of interest to management such as the aforementioned suspicious activity, accidents, and parking violations, which could be realized to be important in the holistic concept of crime prevention.

Being hyper-inclusive, no single set of data exists that rivals CFS for its accuracy. As with any set of statistics, many more desirable possibilities can be derived by performing additional correlations such as sorting crimes by precise location on the property and by times at which they occurred. When more raw data are available in one's database, more meaningful cross-references and correlations are possible. One can consider that some of the fundamental ways people learn about various disciplines are through comparison, trial and error, or cause and effect methods. CFS allows trends or patterns in crime activity to come to light, which aids in the selection of appropriate crime countermeasures and provides for more enlightened comparisons among properties.

Among other considerations that users of CFS should remember, CFS data reflects from the location where a complaint was made, which may or may not be the site of the incident. However, the location and precise nature of the calls can be verified and reliability enhanced when CFS are used in conjunction with the local law enforcement agency's offense or incident reports, which will be discussed in depth later in this chapter.

Some newer CFS systems encode data using the Federal Bureau of Investigation's Uniform Crime Report (UCR) codification system; thus crimes can be easily differentiated from false reports and easily compared to city, state, and national crime levels. Older systems, though, must be converted to UCR through verification with offense reports.

CFS are generally available from the local police department at a reasonable cost. In light of the availability and aforementioned considerations, CFS data can be used effectively to produce a fairly accurate crime history of a property, to distinguish any crime trends or patterns, and to compare properties.

Reliability of CFS

One would be remiss in not realizing that the reliability of CFS has been tested to meet the demands of forecasting crime and other activity that might be of interest to management, such as minor or major traffic accidents, medical emergencies, parking problems, and essentially any situation that may possibly present concerns that would occupy the time of management to solve or rectify. A recent study indicates that CFS over a year's period would have a 90 percent accuracy rate, significantly higher than demographic data in predicting crime in the long run.

OFFENSE REPORTS

More of an expansion of CFS than an independent data source, offense reports, or incident reports as they are sometimes known, should clear up ambiguities and possible inaccuracies through verification of CFS. Sometimes, however, an offense report is generated when police officers discover a crime independent from a call into the 911 emergency system. More precisely, offense reports are the written narrative of a call for service that resulted in an actual crime and include the individual reports of all law enforcement agents, including officers, detectives, and supervisors, who worked the case.

Although availability of offense reports may be limited by law because of inclusion of personal information, victim names, criminal methods, or on-going investigation, property managers should attempt to obtain them from the local law enforcement agency while in the process of conducting crime analysis. Often, however, most states allow the report or a portion of the narrative to be released to the general public upon request. As with all information, property managers should seek access to as much relevant crime information as possible to help make knowledgeable management decisions. By no means should property managers feel that they are in error for not including offense reports when they are not available. On the contrary, one can only do what is reasonable and possible.

UNIFORM CRIME REPORTS

Easily the most exhaustive and geographically comprehensive crime statistics available for the United States, the Federal Bureau of Investigation's Uniform Crime Report (UCR) is also the most well-publicized. Attributing to its reliability as a formidable data source, the UCR uses uniform definitions and elements of crimes in the many law enforcement jurisdictions across the country. UCR delves into this possibility by maintaining data for eight primary crimes listed below, and whose definitions are included in Appendix A at the back of the book.

Violent Crimes:
+ Murder
+ Rape
+ Robbery
+ Aggravated Assault

Property Crimes:
+ Burglary
+ Larceny Theft
+ Motor Vehicle Theft
+ Arson

With the introduction of the FBI's National Incident-Based Reporting System (NIBRS) in the coming years, data on many more offenses will be available to crime analysts, but for now, in-depth information for only these eight is all that is available for consideration. These crimes were selected because they are serious by nature, they occur frequently, they are likely to be reported to law enforcement, they can be confirmed by means of investigation, and they occur across all jurisdictions in the country (O'Brien, 1985). The reliability of these eight crimes may be accredited to these factors.

If CFS are component pieces of a property's crime model, then the UCR is the nation's crime model from which is constructed a larger *reality* to consider. In conjunction with the more concentrated CFS, the UCR allows for strong comparisons: property to city/county, property to state, and property to property.

When using UCR, a few points to be remembered are that it is best to examine violent and property crimes separately, and often the examination of each crime individually is required to thwart an existing or emerging crime trend. Truly, violent and property crimes pose different concerns to management and may require the application of specific crime prevention measures. The UCR hierarchy rule states: In a multiple-offense situation (i.e., one where several offenses are committed at the same time and place), after classifying all index crimes, score only the highest ranking offense, and ignore all others, regardless of the number of offenders and victims. The hierarchy rule does not apply to arson, which is always reported, even in multiple-offense situations. In addition, when larceny and motor vehicle theft occur in a multiple-offense situation, motor vehicle theft is always reported over larceny (FBI, 1966).

As stated earlier, not all crimes are reported to the police and thus will not be included in CFS or UCR. Other considerations that affect the reporting and recording of crime in an area are:

1. Public attitude toward law enforcement and crime. Negative attitudes can at times affect citizens' willingness to report crimes for various reasons, including a feeling that police will not be able to do anything about it or that they do not care
2. Size, population, and demographic composition of an area
3. Economic status and unemployment rate in the area
4. Stability of the population, i.e., the level of transients, commuters, and seasonal population
5. Climate
6. Cultural conditions, i.e., education, recreational habits, and religion of the populace
7. Community (family) values

8. Standards, practices, and relative strength of the law enforcement agency(s)
9. Court's and prosecutor's policies
10. Law enforcement agency(s) administrative effectiveness and efficiency
11. Law enforcement agency(s) investigative effectiveness and efficiency
12. Law enforcement agency(s) accuracy and reporting methods (Texas DPS, 1994)

NATIONAL CRIME VICTIMIZATION SURVEY (NCVS)

The next data set, or measure of crime, is that accumulated through the National Crime Victimization Survey (NCVS), which has been conducted continuously since 1972. Initiated by the United States Census Bureau and the Law Enforcement Assistance Administration (LEAA), the details captured with the NCVS are not typically captured with other crime statistics, namely the UCR.

NCVS data include the characteristics of crime victims, such as age, sex, race, ethnicity, marital status, household income, years at residence, and relationship to the offender. Victim characteristics help property managers recognize those consumers who are at risk and plan for the defense during their visit to the property. One can think of this link to the victim as a furtherance of target-oriented crime prevention goals, and in doing so, not only is that protection planned for the property, but also the lifeblood of the property, customers, tenants, and employees. In rounding out a property's crime picture, management may find such target-based knowledge useful in alliance with the crime-based data of CFS and the UCR. Indeed, the UCR and the NCVS were designed to complement one another to provide the researcher with a functional depiction of crime's attributes. While the UCR has as its primary objective the effective administration and operationalization of crime prevention, be it public or private, the NCVS has the objective to aid in crime prevention by providing practical information about victims, offenders, and the specific traits of a criminal event.

Two counts of crime are derived from the NCVS, one being criminal incidents with a comparable methodology to the UCR, in which only one incident is counted for a continuous sequence of criminal behavior, and the other count being victimizations. Aiding in comparability, the NCVS employs similar crime definitions to those used in the UCR and includes rape, robbery, aggravated assault, burglary, theft, motor vehicle theft, and simple assaults.

Though the UCR and NCVS measure similar crimes, they employ divergent methodologies in arriving at their conclusions. Unlike the UCR's use of actual crime counts, NCVS uses a sampling procedure to develop its findings. Any threats to its integrity as a viable data source are similar to any sample surveys. Where UCR's data are compiled from the actual report of crime to the police or the report of crime from patrol officers, the NCVS data are amassed via survey of approximately 60,000 American households. The sample engaged by the NCVS is large enough to draw conclusions about crime in the United States; however, property managers will find that the sample size is insufficient to draw conclusions to a particular region shy of the whole country. On its own, NCVS may provide little information about crime and what can be done by management to prevent criminal activity, but as an ancillary data set, NCVS adds to the completeness of crime analysis and crime prevention.

DEMOGRAPHIC DATA

Property managers will probably be familiar with demographic data as a marketing tool, but may be unaware of its use as a crime indicator. From the outset, it should be perfectly clear that the authors do not recommend that demographic data be used as an instrument to predict crime. This source has been entertained in the discussion to maintain the integrity of the array of data sources presented.

Though private firms collect demographic data on a much lower geographic level, the U.S. Census Bureau aggregates the bulk of demographic information. The nature of demographics centers on an area's population and its characteristics. Among the more common factors in the census are population counts, socioeconomic levels, education levels, and personal traits of the populous such as age, sex, and race.

Recent debate over the use of demographic data as a crime forecaster has centered on the problems of racial profiling and redlining. Racial profiling describes law enforcement's method of stopping and questioning particular individuals based on personal characteristics, rather than on probable cause. Similarly, private sector companies have been accused of redlining, the refusal to grant service to segments of the population based on demographic data.

Moreover, census information should be used cautiously as it is collected only once every 10 years. Taking into consideration a general axiom of validity that the greater distance between measurement and the present time, it may be further inadvisable not to place too much emphasis on census data as a crime analysis tool. Basic logic aside, census data may not be admissible in a court of law as a crime prediction measure (see foreseeability in Chapter 9).

The U.S. Census Bureau is considering the idea of using sampling methods to arrive at future census counts that may pose even further problems for the property manager using demographics in crime analysis. In summation, there may exist a time when demographic data may prove more useful to the crime analyst, but for now and the foreseeable future, it should not be used as a data source for crime analysis.

Security Reports

A valuable and highly encouraged source of data is in-house security reports (SRs). As the name implies, these are reports of criminal activity and other incidents (parking, loitering, security breaches) that may be of concern to property managers. Management may generate these reports directly or through contracted security companies. The validity of SR data is only as good as the policy that outlines the reporting and recording procedures, the quality of supervision over security personnel, and the verification process used to eliminate subjectivity. Regardless of the quality of their SRs, management should be cautious not to exclude other sources of data and rely solely on in-house security reports. In requiring the collection of SRs, management can stipulate precisely what information is beneficial for their purposes and is contained within each report. Having said that, management should strive to include the following minimum elements:

1. Incident reported
2. Date of incident
3. Time of incident
4. Precise location where the incident occurred on property
5. Victim(s), if any
6. Witness(es), if any
7. Modus Operandi (MO) or Method of Operation used by perpetrator, if any
8. Follow-up investigation(s)
9. Remedy

Arrest Data and Unofficial Crime Statistics

Because crime analysis is based on target-specific crime prevention, rather than concerning themselves with the apprehension of criminals, property managers will find that arrest data are unnecessary for this task. In maintaining the integrity of our crime analysis, only recognized data sources should be included in the analysis to avoid criticism and bias. Also, statistics that are not obtained from an acceptable source may be political in nature.

GEOGRAPHIC LEVELS OF ANALYSIS

As discerned from the circles of control and influence, there exists a hierarchy that denotes the levels of geographic analysis, ranging from the specific to the general. (See Figure 3–1.) For the dual purposes of crime analysis and management, the hierarchy is geared toward being as site-specific as possible. Though one cannot mathematically quantify the importance of each level of geographic analysis, one can distinguish a relationship between, or order of importance for, each level. In defining each level, they have been listed in order of importance, and simultaneously in the order one should be concerned.

Property

Property is the fundamental level of analysis and refers to the singular address of a facility. From crime prevention's vantage, a property is the area over which the manager has absolute control. When

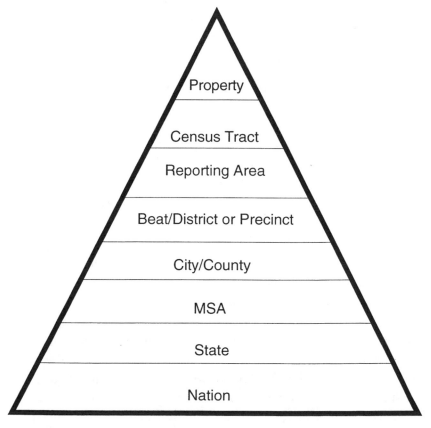

Figure 3–1.   Pyramid/Hierarchy

viewed within the circles of control and influence, property is the innermost circle, or the area over which the property manager has the most ability to regulate. The chief source of crime data for this level is CFS and offense reports, and in-house security reports, if they are available.

Census Tract

Within an inner ring of the circle of influence, census tracts are geographic areas defined by the U.S. Census Bureau for population and demographic purposes. In rare instances, law enforcement agencies have accumulated crime statistics by census tract. Since this occurs infrequently, it is not a standard level of crime analysis, but may be included if the local law enforcement agency maintains data by census tract.

Crime Statistical Reporting Area

A Statistical Reporting Area (RA) is another uncommon level of analysis, and criteria for their creation may diverge significantly across law enforcement jurisdictions. Generally, RAs are small, homogeneous areas created for the sole purpose of supporting crime data collection. When RA data are available, they may be used to assist with the crime analysis of an individual property, and should be considered a standard level of analysis, if available.

Beat, District, or Precinct

Patrol beats are common geographic zones in metropolitan areas that are created by law enforcement agencies to meet their resource allocation objectives—the number of patrol units in an area (beat). Beats are sometimes grouped together and fall under one command center, district, or precinct. The actual land area of beats, the total number of beats, and the number of districts/precincts overseeing the beats can vary considerably in different cities. In metropolitan areas, this is a standard level of analysis and is on an inner ring of our circle of influence. Crime data for these areas are normally available from the local law enforcement agencies on an annual basis and oftentimes maintain crimes similar to those in the UCR.

City/County

A standard level of analysis, city and county data are available from the UCR and encompass crime information for an entire law enforcement jurisdiction. County data include only the crime statistics for rural (unincorporated) areas and not the information for cities within the county. City and county data are on a middle ring of the circle of influence.

Metropolitan Statistical Area (MSA)

Another geographic area created purely for crime statistical purposes, Metropolitan Statistical Areas (MSAs) account for approximately 76 percent of the total U.S. population. MSAs consist of core cities of over 50,000 people and the surrounding suburban regions. This level of analysis exists as an outer ring of the circle of influence.

State

Similar to city and county data, state data can be found in the UCR and include crime information for the entire state. This level of analysis also serves as an outer ring of the circle of influence and details crime statistics for individual states that are often available from a state law enforcement agency.

Nation

On the outermost ring of the circle of influence model lies the country as a whole. Property managers have the least ability to control or influence the crime levels at this level of analysis. Crime statistics for the nation are primarily available through the UCR program, via actual crime information and estimations for the occasional law enforcement jurisdictions that are not involved in the program.

National Incident-Based Reporting System (NIBRS)

Up to this point, the principal sources of data needed for crime analysis have been covered. The future of crime analysis and a new measure of crime is found in the NIBRS, which is currently under testing by the FBI and several law enforcement agencies as a possible replacement for the Uniform Crime Reporting System. As the name implies, NIBRS is an incident-based system, and its trial approach collects data on crime occurrences focusing on each single incident for 46 specific crimes within 22 offense categories. These categories are listed below, and comprehensive data are collected for each incident, known as Group A offenses.

1. Arson
2. Assault Offenses—Aggravated Assault, Simple Assault, Intimidation
3. Bribery
4. Burglary/Breaking and Entering
5. Counterfeiting/Forgery
6. Destruction/Damage/Vandalism of Property
7. Drug/Narcotic Offenses—Drug/Narcotic Violations, Drug Equipment Violations
8. Embezzlement
9. Extortion/Blackmail
10. Fraud Offenses—False Pretenses/Swindle/Confidence Game, Credit Card/Automatic Teller Machine Fraud, Impersonation, Welfare Fraud, Wire Fraud
11. Gambling Offenses—Betting/Wagering, Operating/Promoting/ Assisting Gambling, Gambling Equipment Violations, Sports Tampering
12. Homicide Offenses—Murder and Non-negligent Manslaughter, Negligent Manslaughter, Justifiable Homicide
13. Kidnapping/Abduction
14. Larceny/Theft Offenses—Pocket-picking, Purse-snatching, Shoplifting, Theft from Building, Theft from Coin-Operated

Machine or Device, Theft from Motor Vehicle, Theft of Motor Vehicle Parts or Accessories, All Other Larceny
15. Motor Vehicle Theft
16. Pornography/Obscene Material
17. Prostitution Offenses—Prostitution, Assisting or Promoting Prostitution
18. Robbery
19. Sex Offenses, Forcible—Forcible Rape, Forcible Sodomy, Sexual Assault With an Object, Forcible Fondling
20. Sex Offenses, Non-forcible—Incest, Statutory Rape
21. Stolen Property Offenses (Receiving, etc.)
22. Weapon Law Violations

The NIBRS presents the potential to pinpoint more precise details of individual criminal incidents, entailing when and where crime takes place, as well as the characteristics of its victims and perpetrators. Should NIBRS become the mainstay, it offers to bridge the gap between law enforcement agencies, allow better communication regarding crime trends traversing jurisdictions, and aid in the prevention of crime.

APPLICATION

When last seen, our manager made a list of areas on which to focus his attention; he now sits down to research what materials are needed to fuel his analysis. He takes in all his options, the data sources, and levels of analysis, careful to remember the availability and validity of each.

Wanting to first concentrate on details of the property, he contacts his local police department and requests the CFS for his property's street address. Because he, nor the building's previous manager, required in-house security reports, he must rely solely on CFS for the property's actual crime statistics. Being that this is his first time conducting a crime analysis, he orders CFS for the past five calendar years to help him fully re-create the history of crime on his property since he purchased the building.

A quick call to the police department, and our manager learns that they maintain crime statistics by patrol beat, rather than by reporting areas or census tracts. To attain some understanding of crime in neighboring areas and its influence on his property, our manager requests the city's patrol beat statistics for the previous five calendar years.

He then turns to the Internet for assistance with the larger geographic areas of analysis. Searching for UCRs turns up the FBI's website (*www.fbi.gov*), from which he is able to link to the UCR. He downloads the entire report for the last couple of years and sets it aside until he has received his CFS and beat crime data. The FBI website had UCR information only for the past three years, and in keeping with his five-year standard, he calls the FBI and requests the reports for the remaining two years. To his surprise, he is offered the report in both a written format and as a CD-ROM.

Our manager, recalling the validity of each source, does not order demographic data, but does decide that he would like to get a feel for NCVS' findings. He again turns to the Internet, finds that it is available from the National Criminal Justice Reference Service (NCJRS), and makes a quick call and orders the most recent survey results, *Criminal Victimization in the United States*.

*   *   *   *

Fear of Crime

Perhaps more so than any period of human history, the latter half of the 20th Century may be remembered as the time when innocence was realized to be forever lost amongst a cacophony of demoralized and depraved behavior. During the middle 14th Century, panic was centralized around the black plague, which resulted in the demise of half of Europe's population. Certainly the scare generated by the plague was warranted, as preventive measures were seemingly limited to quarantine and evacuation. No reliable cure could be found.

Subsequent history shows how the concern of the populace succumbed to that of wars and pestilence that augmented the landscape under dire circumstances. This trend of designing one's life around the threat of the day has continued on and become the paramount catalyst for the overall schematic of modern lifestyle. So pervasive is the threat that people often live without consciously remembering it, just simply acting on it.

Since the end of the second world war, American life has been assaulted by the criminal element. To be sure, crime existed before, but not at the level or in the indiscriminate manner in which it operates today. In the 1930s, organized crime was romanticized by the likes of Al Capone, Baby Face Nelson, Bonnie Parker and Clyde Barrow. The randomness of crime was actually brought to the forefront of concern after World War II, when the growth of urban environments transpired more so than perhaps any other time in history. With that growth came a dilution of social institutions that traditionally restricted behavior. This included the breakdown of the American family, the increasing responsibility of schools to control behavior, the weakening of the church, the pressures of the economy, the politicization of crime, and a general imbalance among these institutions (Messner and Rosenfeld, 1994). Further blame for increasing crime has been laid at the doorsteps of unemployment rates, growing disunity in communities, and the wholesale glamorization of crime in the media.

What has resulted is that fear of crime has blossomed into one, if not the primary, reason why people live where they do and why they constantly seek improved living arrangements. Intangibly, fear of crime has affected the mindset of the population and tapped into the darker side of the human imagination, where this concern has built exponentially into a collective paranoia. As it stands, entire generations are growing up with the inevitability of becoming crime victims, thus perpetuating a notion of hopelessness and despair.

This reality is not provided by delusionary circumstances. Though it is not easily quantifiable, nor officially measured, the property manager must constantly evaluate the fear of crime's effects on the quality of life. As reported in studies examining such matters, the deluge of crime on life is an increasing concern for all Americans, spurred on by accounts of personal victimization, workplace violence, and the recent preponderance of shootings in schools. Surveys have indicated that three-quarters of Americans are willing to forfeit basic civil liberties in an effort to further provide for personal security, and that they have been found to harbor a deeper fear of crime and its consequences than of more frequent automobile accidents, heart disease, or cancer. No one person's fear can be rationalized exactly the same, though recent surveys have shown some interesting commonalities, such as exhibiting a greater fear of car-jacking than aggravated assault, robbery, or murder, even though it occurs less frequently (Flanagan and Longmire, 1996). One might ponder the root of this apprehension as the quantity of media coverage regarding this crime has increased.

Personally, I remember one summer night hearing a neighbor screaming out in terror. Briefly, I entertained the thought of investigating the matter, but my own fear prevented me from doing so. As I later found out, my neighbors, who had returned from out of town, had been robbed at gunpoint.

A front yard chat with my neighbor a week later provided the facts of the night in question. They had driven straight from the airport to our suburban neighborhood, and upon pulling into their driveway, were followed in by a car of men. These men quickly exited their vehicle and ran up to greet my neighbors with pistols, demanding money and jewelry. The scream I heard was my neighbor warning her 12-year-old son to remain in the house. Fortunately, no one was injured, save for my neighbors' mental anguish . . . and mine. Their son had made it back inside and called the police, who later apprehended the criminals, though failed to recover the valuables.

The impetus for the chat with my neighbor was that I had noticed a newly posted "for sale" sign on their lawn. They were moving. The neighborhood had always enjoyed a reputation of being a safe haven from such incidents, and its residents had built a trust around that fact. As remote and isolated as the incident was in relation to the history of the area, my neighbors had lost faith in the covenant between neighborhood and resident. They were moving away. My neighbor told me that he realized something could happen anywhere else, but the fact remained that those particular criminals knew where they lived and he feared reprisal. As illogical as his thinking may have been, his concern for his family's well-being was not satisfied by the odds against a repeat occurrence. The neighborhood had lost a good resident. I had lost a fine neighbor.

There were many victims that night, some in larger ways than others, but victims nonetheless. My own experience with this incident was not to end with my neighbor's departure. I found myself doubly aware of crime and the potential risks not just in the neighborhood, but everywhere. My own innocence had been violated, and I was a changed man. My daily habits changed, I found myself suspicious of being followed, my caution at nighttime bordered on a disorder, and I had thought about carrying a weapon. It took me several years to realize that the latter would bring nothing but trouble and that by using a weapon, my life would be further altered if my actions were premature and unsupported by fact.

Now that crime occupies such a prominent place in our lives, there is no way that it can be casually forgotten. In fact, the only casual aspect is that every year as the crime rates fluctuate and more heinous crimes are committed, the collective conscience of society grows that much more jaded. The local evening news devotes one-third of its programming time to detailing new innovations in cruelty and inhumanity. It brings to our attention nightly, a parade of gruesome images, wounded victims, and unrepentant perpetrators, and it wears on us to such a degree that it doesn't matter any more.

Or does it?

4

Site-Specific Crime Analysis: From Theory to Application

RATIONALITY

What goes through one's mind when considering rationality? Surely the concept itself is almost like an undefinable word, which while a textbook definition may be applicable to a point, it may not be fully grasped without myriad examples illustrating its meaning. Such is the concept of rationality. When mere words fail to attain the all-encompassing direction and aesthetic sought, one often retreats with the vacant conclusion of circular reasoning. It's rational, because it is rational. But, the concept of rationality is plagued by subjectivity. No two views of a decision or work based in reason can be precisely understood. To make a generalization that types of people with same or similar interests tend to rationalize in the same exact way or even in the same direction, is to make a grave mistake. Unless one can acquire the power to enter another's mind and discern between their own thinking and another's, one cannot hope to realize the mindset they are in when making a certain decision or performing an act. They are locked outside of the human consciousness save for their own, but the more one knows about rationality and one's own personal process of reasoning, based on observation, more can be learned about human behavior and how to provide for it in some measure as a society.

At the heart of rationality is reason. Perhaps the most famous and widely quoted example is, "I think, therefore I am." Within that statement lies a plethora of reason backed by concrete fact. A person can look down at his or her own body and see a figure—an irrefutable proof of existence.

While basic, the concept of rationality and reason is so often taken for granted that it scarcely seems appreciable, but it is a tenet of existence itself and not exclusive to humans. On a lesser platform, animals can sense both danger and kindness and have the innate ability to differentiate when circumstances are optimized. One can also see that reasoning skills are further called upon the more advanced the individual becomes. The reasoning and rationality of children certainly cannot be compared to that of adults with a wealth of experience to draw on and an advanced intelligence to guide them.

Earlier in this volume, how chess players cogitate over potential moves was discussed. Truly theirs is a pastime (at the height of that discipline an occupation bordering on devotion) that endeavors toward a monumental peak of rationality on multiple levels. During a tournament game of chess, a player must rationalize:

1. within his or her own mind;
2. in relation to the objectivity of the game;
3. the facts offered by the positioning of the pieces and available moves;
4. in comparison or contrast to the opponent across the board.

Their chore is made doubly difficult by the presence of second-guessing, strategic deception, previous history in familiar tactical positions, and previous history playing against a particular opponent. Within these individual challenges remains the struggle for survival and superiority of the game itself. In a game of decisions, sometimes a decision needs to be made whether to be made at all or how much time will be expended in doing so. In tournament games, time is of the essence and therefore limits the scope of each move. A person must decide to channel his or her energies into deep analysis at that particular juncture of the game or decide that time may be better spent later on in the game. In making such a decision, a player takes into consideration how much time is remaining on the clock and how many moves need to be reached before a certain point (oftentimes tournament chess games mandate that the first 40 moves be made within a two-hour time constraint, with each subsequent 10 moves being made within each additional hour) or time control, how much time remains on the opponent's clock, the relative complexity of the current position, material advantages or disadvantages, spatial advantages or disadvantages, mental fatigue, and any other factors that may enter into a player's thinking. In making such a decision, the person will have mentally stated the factors and attached values to them. Once processed, he or she can weigh relative values until a conclusion has been reached. At that point, an emotional or subjective bond can be formed around that decision, or what in lay terms is often referred to as a gut feeling. Hindsight will show that the judgment was correct or incorrect, but nevertheless the process has come to fruition, but in self-examination as well as observation of others, rationalizations may be improved upon.

As suggested, rationality is not a special skill that is acquired; it is inherent in human nature and operates within the individual in such a way that in development, comparing one's reasoning skills to another's is an exercise in futility. One can hope to grow within one's self and expectations. Everyday decisions are made based on information gathered.

How should I get to work this morning? Well, it's Monday, traffic on the freeway will be heavy up to mid-town and then it thins out from there on in. If I can deal with sitting in bumper-to-bumper traffic for 10 miles, I'll be able to have an easy drive during the second half of the drive. On the other hand, I can take side streets behind the mall and catch the mid-town entrance to the freeway and not sit in traffic on the freeway. But, there are about 10 stoplights on the side streets no matter which ones I take, and those lights back up a few minutes apiece. If there is a stalled car on the way in to work, I can always take another side street, whereas if I'm on the freeway, there are no alternate routes.

Certainly people rationalize their activities much in the same manner, albeit without all the exposed detail. Granted that detail is intact in our mind, it was simplified in compressed cognitive templates that represent knowledge or experience.

As difficult as it may seem, if a person can be mindful to explore our thought patterns, he or she will find that our reasoning skills come into play in just about every activity we do or even consider. To trace the choices faced within even a single conscious hour would be near impossible to inventory, and then one would need to rationalize the purpose of undertaking the challenge.

ROUTINE

Every bit as difficult to quantify is the concept of routine. In fact, the very nature of routine is to assimilate, to appear customary and operate according to procedure. Like rationality, routines are something that inhabit every human being (and some other species as well), but unlike rationality, the concept of routine is not a concept whose results can be measured as directly. However, hard work and adherence to a strict regimen can provide one with the basis for success on a given project. Routines are easier to trace as they leave their tracks in their wake.

A mother of three wakes up at 6 a.m. every weekday morning and starts the coffee pot. While the coffee is brewing, she selects something to wear to work that day. She takes her coffee at the kitchen table, where she peruses the newspaper. By 7 a.m., her children are stirring, she starts breakfast for them, and then she showers and goes about furthering herself for work. Almost ready for work, she urges her children to prepare for school. Having collected her purse and car keys, she ushers her children to the car for the drive to work and school. As each child is dropped off at their respective schools, she doles out lunch money and kisses them goodbye for the day. By 8:15, she leaves the neighborhood and makes her way to work, where she arrives somewhere in the area of 9 a.m.

Routines can develop from contentment or necessity or a synthesis of both to form what can be construed as stability. Though routines themselves do not provide material security, they can work as a comfort level from which one can derive some expectations. How do routines begin? One could say that in a given situation, an event occurs and upon repetition, a functional technique or procedure is established. As it is functional and regarded as successful, a person is prone to stick with it until it is proven otherwise or the situation changes or initiates change. Routines tend to have much in common with Kepler's first law of physics, which states, "An object at rest tends to remain at rest unless acted upon by another force." A solid, comfortable routine tends to remain in place; an overwhelming majority of Americans can no doubt attest to this fact.

The daily routine has become such a hallmark in American life that we can find references scattered throughout popular culture from literature, television, and motion pictures. It has been both embraced and lampooned, but above all been realized and accepted. Two questions to ask: Do we ask too much from our routines? Can a routine dull the senses or trivialize matters that should be kept on high priority, like that of flying an airplane? Certainly, problems do occur with routine-intensive tasks, such as those of air traffic controllers. While the critical and precise nature of the job contributes a good deal of the stress accumulated, some blame surely falls on their routines dulling the senses in times when alertness is of the utmost importance. Like many other concepts, it can be agreed that when managed in moderation, routines serve people well, but when blindly adhered to, they have the propensity to do great harm.

SYNTHESIS

Now that the concepts of routine and rationality have been examined, how do the two come together? An example from the sport of baseball is summoned. Like the dilemma of the chess player, the reasoning skills used are of the highest order, as one considers the thoughts of a big league manager and his bench coach, their pitcher, and catcher.

With their team up by one run in the bottom half of the ninth inning and an opposing runner on first base, no one out, and the opposing team's three best hitters due up at bat, the team attempts to plot out a strategy based on the tendencies of the forthcoming hitters, the tendencies of the opposing manager, and the chances of success for either team within the framework of the game situation.

As the first of the opposing trio of hitters steps into the batter's box, the bench coach turns to the manager and mentions that the runner on first base does not run well, but in this desperate situation may be given the green light to steal second base. Among other information offered by the bench coach, the runner on first does not read pitchers well, meaning he cannot pick up on the pitcher's foot work enough to tell if he is throwing straight to the plate or if he will turn suddenly and toss the ball to first base for a pick-off play. The manager weighs this new information and signals for the pitcher to keep the base runner close to the bag by frequently looking the runner back to the bag. The manager also knows that his pitcher has a good slide-step move, which is that the pitcher can utilize a low leg raise in his pitch delivery that further confuses a base runner trying to read his movements. The batter, the bench coach informs, while being a good hitter, is prone to chasing low fastballs just out of the strike zone. Again signals are transmitted to the field. After a few tosses to first, the pitcher throws a curve ball low and away. The batter takes the pitch and watches as the referee judges it a ball. The pitcher, beginning his delivery from his belt so as to prepare for a pick-off move to first base, cannot quite match the velocity he would ordinarily enjoy when utilizing a full wind up, so as a result his fastball will not be up to optimal speed. Still looking the runner on first base back to the bag, the pitcher delivers a deceptive change-of-pace pitch that is taken for a strike. Mustering his energy, the pitcher throws a fastball that tails just out of the strike zone and is unsuccessfully pursued, wildly, by the batter. The count is now one ball, two strikes.

Not wanting to back the hitter into a corner and feed him a pitch right over the plate, the pitcher wastes a pitch (called for by the catcher), which sails way inside to brush the batter back off the plate. The intention is that if a batter is more timid and backed off the plate, the goal of owning the outside portion of the plate can be reached. Since this is the most predominant weakness of that particular hitter, this strategy seems sound. After a few more close plays at first base (the base runner has to scamper back from the position he has advanced to in his leadoff from the bag), the pitcher throws a fastball with tailing movement toward the outside of the plate. Since the hitter is 6'3" and likes to extend his arms on balls thrown to the outside (another tidbit of scouting information), he finds the temptation too strong to pass up and swings for the fences. But as the swing is completed, the only sound is that of the baseball against the back of the catcher's glove. One out, two to go.

The manager then trots out to the mound and is met by the catcher. The trio decides to try and induce an inning-ending double play by offering ground ball pitches, which will entail the infield to shift around the diamond to maintain necessary range to accommodate the double play. The manager signals to his shortstop to move back a few steps and in toward second base and for the second baseman to do the same on the right side. The pitcher and catcher decide to throw sliders low and away, and fastballs high and in on the strike zone to offer contrast and to better portray the outside pitches as being desirable to take a swing. Continuous looks back to first base seem to suggest that the runner on first base has abandoned all hopes of stealing second base, but with a double play a very real possibility, the opposing manager could signal for a steal if only to break up a double play with a hard slide into second base by the base runner (which would inhibit the throw by either the second baseman or the shortstop). The first pitch is a fastball high and in, and is taken for a ball. The hitter barely flinches. Next pitch is a slider away, and the hitter flails away vainly, actually losing his balance for a half second. The catcher notices that the lack of attention paid to the runner on first base has given the runner renewed ideas about stealing second, so the catcher signals for a fastball well outside. Before the pitch, the catcher slyly sets up in his crouched stance to the outside of the plate. The pitcher delivers, and the hitter, seeing that the pitch is extraordinarily outside, does not even think about swinging. Immediately, the catcher pulls in the pitch, stands up, and throws in a single motion toward first base. A fine sweeping tag applied by the first baseman to the base runner on first results in the runner being called out. Two outs. The count on the hitter is 2–1. The scouting report on the hitter also shows that he will swing at almost anything when the count is in his favor, which it happens to be.

With the base runner on first erased, there is obviously a greater urgency for the opposing team to score a run, so the catcher decides to make things interesting and calls for a rising fastball. A rising fastball is thrown with the fingers across the thickest part of the ball and when thrown actually rises upward as it reaches the plate rather than at the customary downward plane. The pitcher responds by delivering a beautiful pitch that causes the hitter to swing from his heels at a seemingly ideal pitch, but the rising motion denies him any solid contact between the bat and the ball. The count is now 2–2.

The manager and bench coach had things in motion initially, but have now decided to allow the catcher to continue as field general as he has done an outstanding job thus far. The catcher thinks about how the umpire has called the game, quite consistently he decides, and since a fair share of inside pitches have resulted in called strikes, decides to chance it by calling for a change-of-pace pitch toward the inside. His rationale: If the pitch is called a ball, then the count is 3–2, and his team has another chance to pitch to this hitter. If it is put into play, the positioning of the ball is such that he would likely only be able to make cursory contact with the ball, and the infield should be able to make the conservative play at first base. Acquiescing to the catcher, the pitcher nods in agreement and winds up and brilliantly locates the pitch. The catcher leaves his glove in the precise position used to catch it so the umpire has a better frame of reference to judge the pitch. The strategy works, and the umpire calls strike three. Three outs. Game over.

Every day people execute routines thoughtlessly, with no idea that someone could be taking careful note of their each and every move. But people do, and more importantly, criminals do. Some criminals have made a career of assailing polite society by observing its very nature and exploiting weaknesses they may find. In this chapter, we will examine how such a thing could happen and how criminals utilize rational judgment to carry out such machinations.

Throughout this text, the concept of property-specific or target-oriented crime analysis and the data used to accomplish such evaluations have become intimately familiar. There has been no discussion of criminal motivation; instead the importance of the property's criminal career has been stressed, rather than the persons. Property managers shouldn't take on the role of psychologist and concern themselves with the criminal mind; instead they should work to analyze their property's criminal opportunities. Conventional criminologists have worked tirelessly toward stopping criminals from offending, yet after years of effort, a solution is not in hand. The time is ripe for a new approach, target-oriented crime prevention. Like parents creating a safe, hazard-free environment for children to play, property managers can create a safe environment for consumers. In managing these environments, a property manager's goal is to balance the freedom and needs of customers and tenants while actively blocking opportunities for crime by would-be offenders.

Gone are the days when the job of crime prevention fell solely to the police. Rapid increases in the nation's crime rates during the '60s, '70s, and '80s can be attributed to a myriad of factors. The consequence, however, is the same: Law enforcement operating by itself cannot bring crime down to pre-1960 levels. Only through a joint effort of the police, property managers, and citizens does society have a chance of creating a safer country. The police have recognized this, and many police departments have implemented community-oriented policing programs.

Effective property managers are the failsafe for those crimes that the police could not prevent. Who among society is best able to monitor behavior in different places? On public streets, society's rules are enforced via the police. In public schools, teachers and principals have the ability to safeguard against crime. In hotels, apartments, stores, banks, and gas stations, property managers are best able to regulate behavior. Working within their own domains, property managers have the best ability to influence behavior and, done effectively, crime rates will fall.

Inventors study past research and proven correlations to build on, and the task of crime analysis and prevention is no different. This text has drawn upon the work of several well-developed perspectives of crime and prevention, consisting of Rational Choice, Routine Activity, Crime Pattern, and Situational Crime Prevention. These theories have laid the foundation for the development of a functional crime analysis approach and for the creation of certain techniques for reducing crime. It is critical to understand the basic principles of these perspectives, thus Rational Choice, Routine Activity, Crime Pattern, and Situational Crime Prevention are examined.

RATIONAL CHOICE

Criminals act rationally when planning a crime by weighing the risks, rewards, and efforts needed to commit their transgressions. The rational choice crime perspective, developed in the United Kingdom by Ronald V. Clarke, explains a criminal's decision-making process for selecting targets and how managers of these targets can block criminal opportunities. Like anybody, a criminal's rationality may be limited by time, intelligence, and accuracy of information. Because the reasoning criminal is logical, his or her behavior can be explained, predicted, and controlled. Rather than the conventional deterrent of punishment, this perspective advocates blocking criminal opportunities, or target hardening, as the primary deterrent to crime.

SPECIFIC CRIME EMPHASIS

Rational choice illustrates how a criminal's quest for money, power, status, or excitement may be hindered by an effective crime prevention program built on property- and crime-specific analysis. To ensure the program's effectiveness, crime should be studied at the property level, with incidents categorized by the target of crime (based on the criminal's expected gain), the level of risk to that asset, and the value of that asset should it be lost to crime, natural disaster, or another event.

As learned in Chapter 3, the compilation of certain data is a prerequisite to fully understand the crime problem. Property managers should evaluate the circumstances that facilitated criminal incidents and, in an efficient and planned manner, impede those crime opportunities.

IMPLICATIONS FOR CRIME PREVENTION

An offender's decision to commit a crime can be controlled through the presence of countermeasures on a property, and in some cases, the criminal's behavior may be re-directed by the mere perception of security. Crime prevention measures, tangible or otherwise, must make it clear to a criminal that there is a high likelihood of apprehension and that punishment, or pain, will follow their behavior.

As mentioned previously, the value of assets needs to be calculated to select appropriate, cost-effective, commensurate countermeasures. Obviously, a manager of a warehouse would not be expected to allocate $5,000 for a CCTV system to protect merchandise worth $3,000.

Rational choice theory has an application component known as situational crime prevention, which concludes that specific criminal events have a set of traits that are used to develop appropriate crime prevention measures. As an application, situational crime prevention has already developed a set of techniques to harden targets or block criminal opportunities. This topic will be addressed in Chapter 7 (Crime Prevention Programs).

ROUTINE ACTIVITY

Those familiar with serial criminals will recognize that they usually operate in a consistent manner, that is they have a Modus Operandi (MO or method of operation) that is common to most, if not all, their crimes. England's infamous killer, Jack the Ripper, had a routine of choosing his victims from the same London pub, where he stalked them to their homes, ultimately leading to their deaths. What one can learn from this is that by inquiring into typical practices on and around a given property, opportunities for undesirable activity will be uncovered.

Complementary to rational choice is routine activity theory, which demonstrates the manner in which criminals find suitable targets and opportunities during the course of their daily actions and social interactions. Routine activity is concerned with what occurs when targets and offenders converge in time and space. Determining people's routine activities on and around a facility helps predict criminal and non-criminal behavior. Specifically, crime opportunities can be discovered through a purposeful search of available routes to and through a property and the targets along or just off those routes.

The intersection of targets and offenders in time and space in itself does not create crime. Other elements are necessary. First, the offender must be motivated to commit an illegal act and be without an individual who can control his or her actions (routine activity calls this person a handler). Second, the place where the uncontrolled, motivated offender and a suitable target meet must be absent an effective guardian, a person who increases the risk to the criminal. Broken down into its minimal components, the following must be present for a crime to occur:

1. Motivated offender—a person ready and willing to commit a crime.

2. Absent or ineffective handler—a person who influences the behavior of the offender. Handlers include parents, relatives, friends, teachers, employers, etc.
3. Suitable target—a person or asset that is of value to an offender.
4. Absent or ineffective guardian—a person who protects the target from harm. Guardians include police, parents, relatives, friends, and property managers.
5. Time—a period for the first four ingredients to come together.
6. Space—a place for the first four ingredients to cross paths.

Once there is an understanding of these elements, one can move on to consider the various types of crime options available to eliminate one or more ingredients to prevent crime.

SPECIFIC CRIME EMPHASIS

It is important to gain complete understanding of the types of crime that are affecting the property in order to select the crime prevention measures to deter those crimes. "Detailed local analysis is the best way to learn how crime reaches people (Felson and Clarke, 1997)." Routine activity illustrates that there are four types of crime to which targets may be subjected:

1. Exploitive crimes are those where one or more offenders injure or kill a person or seize or damage another's property. Index crimes (murder, rape, robbery, aggravated assault, burglary, theft, motor vehicle theft, arson) exemplify this predatory type of crime.
2. Mutualistic crimes involve two people or groups engaged in complementary roles of crime. Examples are gambling, prostitution, and drug purchases.
3. Competitive crimes are those where two people or groups act in the same capacity and usually entail a physical conflict against each other.
4. Individualistic crimes are illegal acts committed by a sole offender and are usually referred to as victimless crimes. This

category of crime may be exemplified by drug use and suicide (Felson and Clarke, 1997).

IMPLICATIONS FOR CRIME PREVENTION

Examining routine activities on and around a property, recognizing criminal opportunities, specifically the ingredients of crime, and understanding the types of crime that may affect a property shed light for those seeking to reduce crime. A property manager has the unique ability to limit and regulate the routines of people on the property, while being cautious to avoid impeding normal business operations or violating any person's rights. "Just as unseen traffic engineers do us all a good deed by designing streets and intersections to minimize citizen danger, so can architects, planners, and facility managers quietly and unobtrusively help prevent crime victimization (Felson and Clarke, 1997)."

CONCLUSION

Rational choice and routine activity provide the framework to create a crime prevention program geared toward reducing the actual rate of crime on a property, reducing the fear of crime on the part of the consumers, and increasing the quality of life on the property. The culmination of these two perspectives form the empirical basis of the crime analysis methodology described in the next chapter. Before seeking an application scenario of concepts described in this chapter, some key generalizations should be reviewed:

+ Crime is not random, nor uniform.
+ Crime is patterned and predictable.
+ Crime is committed by reasoning criminals.
+ Crime is the end result of a decision-making process.
+ Crime opportunities are actively and passively sought during routine activities.

♦ Crime occurs when motivated offenders with ineffective or non-existent handlers converge in time and space with suitable targets with ineffective or non-existent guardians.

Crime can be prevented by removing one of its ingredients. For property managers this means blocking opportunities by using the following:

1. Regulating behavior at the site (active and effective guardianship).
2. Using appropriate crime prevention measures to increase an offender's actual or perceived risk (decreasing motivation).
3. Encouraging handlers to visit the site with potential offenders (active handling).
4. Some combination of the above.

5

By-Products of Crime Analysis and Prevention

There are several by-products of effective crime prevention worth noting and anticipating. The first of these is the possibility of non-violent criminal behavior escalating into a violent episode. Violence escalation may occur when security personnel, police officers, property managers, or another person interrupts a criminal during the commission of a crime. In a technical manner, escalation can be defined as a single crime in progress that is interrupted because one or more victims or witnesses have confronted the offender during the commission of the offense wherein, following the interruption, a more serious crime is committed against either the victim or witness. This phenomenon is actually quite rare, as more often than not, criminals will attempt flight before fight. Despite the rarity of the phenomenon itself, the relevance of violence escalation lies in the prevalence of factors that cause escalation. It is a significant concern for property managers because effective crime countermeasures do increase the likelihood of crimes being thwarted in progress, thereby increasing the chances for violent behavior. Those who are designated to intervene in criminal behavior should be prepared, trained, and equipped for any dangers that may arise.

More appropriately, property managers should ask the question, What could we do to prevent violence when we see the signs? Retail loss prevention personnel who confront shoplifters regularly are usually well trained in watching for the signs of possible violence, and property managers as a whole should also be able to identify and avoid factors that may lead to violence escalation.

The identification of violence escalation factors have become considerably more important in light of current trends of violence in schools and in the workplace. Shootings at schools, such as recent incidents in Jonesboro, Arkansas, and at Columbine High School in Littleton, Colorado, are clear examples of verbal threats and physical confrontations escalating into murders and assaults. Workplace violence is also a growing concern in America as workers become more disillusioned by the demands of supervisors, customers, and fellow employees. "Violence by workers is invariably in response to frustration in the workplace (Souryal, 1998)." Evidence of workplace violence can be found across the nation, including in U.S. post offices, where shootings have occurred with such frequency that the phenomenon has been labeled "going postal."

Violence escalation is a serious matter; however, it is not a common phenomenon. One or more factors, which can cause escalation, are usually associated with all criminal activity. Because of the frequency of these factors in crime, they are important to identify and examine in efforts to increase the probability of violence prevention. For a number of reasons, even the most mild-mannered criminals may become prone to violence when confronted. Instability may be rooted in physical or mental illness, emotional distress, substance abuse, stress, or anger. Non-verbal cues will provide the most valuable information into the person's intentions, though the power of empathetic listening should not be underestimated.

The level to which management or security personnel can prevent or control violent behavior depends on their ability to quickly and accurately assess the situation, recognize key warning signs, and respond appropriately without exacerbating the situation. It should be noted that unless personnel are adequately trained in responding to violence, no attempt should be made to control a potentially dangerous situation.

Two recent studies of violence escalation by a group of crime prevention practitioners and a researcher examining school violence identified a number of factors that may increase the probability of violence. These factors include the use of a weapon by the criminal, police interruption of the crime, the existence of a relationship between the offender and victim, and confrontation of the perpetrator by the victim or a witness.

The study conducted by the group of crime prevention practitioners found that only 4 percent of crimes escalated in the level of violence or into violence, leaving 95 percent of crimes unchanged while 1 percent de-escalated. It is important to look at each crime separately to determine its escalation tendency in efforts to reduce the opportunity for these crimes to occur and to reduce their escalation probability. (see Table 5–1.)

Noticeably absent from the list of crimes is murder because, under the hierarchy of crimes described in Chapter 3, murder cannot escalate, as it is the highest crime in the hierarchy. As seen in the following table, more rapes escalated into violence or in the level of violence used to complete the crime than any other crime.

Generally, weapon use in crime does not guarantee that actual violence will result. In only a very small portion of crimes does violence erupt or increase when a weapon is introduced into the equation. In fact, more crimes escalated when a weapon was not used in the crime. Despite the narrow likelihood of violence escalating, property managers should still do what they can to prevent illegal weapons on their properties.

Table 5–1   Crime Escalation Rates.

Rape	12.5%
Robbery	3.1%
Aggravated Assault	3.7%
Burglary	2.0%
Theft	6.6%
Auto Theft	0.8%

One of the most common defenses in civil liability cases is the inability to prevent or even deter acquaintance crimes. Acquaintance offenses are those crimes in which the offender and victim are related in some way, usually intimately. Therefore, the suspect-victim relationship becomes an important variable for analysis.

One of the toughest situations property managers or their designated security personnel may find themselves in is a confrontation between people that know each other. When violence does occur, the escalation of a domestic dispute is usually quite rapid and difficult to prevent in the short term. On the other hand, proper countermeasures will help reduce escalation over the long run.

When police officers interrupt a crime in progress, one would tend to believe that the result would be a rapid de-escalation of any violence. To the contrary, police interruption causes much more escalation than de-escalation. Property managers should consider this when deciding on security or police officers to provide a human presence on a property.

A primary concern for property managers is that a theft or shoplifting will develop into a violent crime when the criminal is confronted. Certain crimes, especially property crimes, are prone to escalation when the victim confronts the perpetrator of a crime. For the property manager, this would be a clear indication that extreme caution should be exercised when confronting people stealing from the property.

DISPLACEMENT

The next by-product of effective crime prevention is the phenomenon of displacement, where crimes occur at another location where crime prevention measures are lacking or non-existent. Crime displacement has been heavily debated in academic circles with no particular prevailing viewpoint. Only effective crime prevention can cause displacement, thus it should be of minor concern for property managers as the objective is to prevent crime on a particular property, and should displacement occur, the crime will shift to another

Table 5–2   The Six Most Commonly Discussed Types of Displacement.

Type	Description
Temporal	Offenders shift the timing of their offenses to different hours of the day or days of the week when offending is seen as less risky.
Target	Offenders forsake well-protected targets and focus their efforts on more vulnerable ones.
Spatial	Offenders move away from the areas in which crime has become more difficult to commit, and begin to commit unlawful acts in another location.
Tactical	Offenders change the tactics they use to commit a crime in order to circumvent an obstacle designed to thwart them.
Perpetrator	As the offenders who typically commit certain offenses are either arrested or decide to desist from it, other offenders take their place.
Type of Crime	Offenders respond to the blocking of one specific form of crime by committing entirely different types of offenses.

location. Table 5–2 outlines the types of displacement to ensure completeness of this volume (Clarke and Felson, 1993).

DIFFUSION OF BENEFITS

Displacement and violence escalation are not the sole reported side effects of crime prevention. At the other end of the spectrum, crime prevention can serve those who are not its direct or intended beneficiaries. The goodness of crime prevention may spread to neighboring properties through diffusion of benefits, a process by which security measures implemented at one property may prevent crime at another location, usually a neighboring property. An obvious example of this is lighting. A property that has lighting cannot wholly contain it to its own property—that light will also fall on properties and streets that surround the hardened property.

CONCLUSION

Individual property managers should be encouraged by diffusion of benefits, while at the same time, not discouraged by crime displacement. In a perfect world, all property managers would implement effective crime prevention, and crime will not be displaced. On the other hand, violence escalation does pose threats and can be reduced using various violence prevention methods. Training programs should be implemented for teachers, parents, and police officers because these people may come in contact with students during a confrontation. With 18 percent of the incidents occurring in the classroom, this training would likely be most useful for teachers. Furthermore, the training needs to emphasize conflict resolution in an effort to avoid violent episodes. Other solutions may lie in the schools' policies that teach social skills and punish even the least serious offenses. Swift, certain, and just punishment for violation of school policies is likely to reduce the number of offenses. Finally, peer mediation groups can be created to allow students to resolve situations amongst themselves without pressure from adults (Lockwood, 1997).

In light of the violence escalation studies, property managers can emphasize property crime prevention as a conduit to violent crime prevention. This proactive approach will accomplish three goals. First, civil liability from claims of negligent or inadequate security will be significantly reduced, though the number of lawsuits filed will not likely be affected. Second, property managers will improve consumer satisfaction by reducing fear of crime on their property. Consequently, properties will increase profitability because consumers will be more willing to frequent the properties to spend their money. Third, property managers can decrease operating costs. Security consumes much of a property manager's budget because security and prevention programs are often ineffective, outdated, or otherwise non-existent. By implementing a program based on tested research, property managers can deliver what they are legally obligated to provide in protecting their consumers from harm or danger.

Furthermore, a tested, site-specific prevention program is more cost effective than a universally applied or haphazard program.

APPLICATION: FICTIONAL SCENARIO

Considering what he has learned about routine activity, rationality, violence escalation, displacement, and diffusion of benefits, our manager makes another round of the property, a slower, more deliberate examination scanning possible scenarios where security may be breached and for opportunities to forecast how it could happen. To accomplish this, he channels the dark side of his conscious self and looks for trouble areas just as if he were the perpetrator. Most of the crime, he can imagine, will occur in the parking garage; our manager begins there:

Passing by the building on my way back into the city, I might notice an attractive proposition, perhaps an unaccompanied female or aloof male whom I may decide to take advantage of. I pass by this way almost every day. I see how the people are dressed and the kinds of cars they drive. There is definitely something worth looking into at this property.

On the main street, from a car or on foot, I could move to the sidewalk and snatch someone's purse or briefcase, possibly take other valuables that seem worth the effort. If I wanted a greater payoff, I'll need to get to the parking garage. I could approach from the sidewalk and get inside by vaulting the retaining wall on the ground floor (I can see that it's only four feet high) or walking through one of the vehicle entrances (there is no security officer or access gate to stop me). Once inside, I could steal a car or at the very least break into one of the cars and make off with any valuables left there. Later in the evening, I'll have the cover of darkness on my side. If I was a sex offender, I could perpetrate such a crime with considerably more ease than in daylight. I have not seen cameras or anyone overseeing the parking garage, but I will assume that someone is at least watching from a distance. And if by chance I am seen, dressed casually the way

I am, I'll stand out against the kinds of people I have seen in here when I've cut through the garage to get to the main street. If I have to run, it will be in the direction of Main Street, where I will stand a good chance of mixing in with the crowd. Should I not have to flee, there are numerous other places to hide such as the stairwells, beneath cars, and dark corners.

The walkway between the parking garage and the building is another place I might go to cash in on a score. Lining the walkway is a row of tall, dense bushes. I could fit easily within the brush and watch people coming and going until the opportunity is ripe for my move.

Around the side of the building there is a service door where I've seen people coming and going and know that it is often left open. I could quietly slip inside and no one would know. As for people entering and exiting, I could hide behind the bushes around that area, jump out and surprise them, and be off onto the side street and away before they knew what hit them. This would be an easier target than the front entrance because it has less traffic and is closer to the main street. Also, there is a building under construction on that side that I could use to give someone pursuing me the slip.

Inside the building, our manager adjusts his thinking to that of a more experienced criminal, one who is trained in more complex crimes, is more patient, and whose thinking is more sublime:

There is a universal visibility inside the building that I must be careful of, there is so much open space, people are entering and exiting their individual suites and utilizing conference rooms, restrooms, utility closets—I need to act like I belong. This is much closer to people's livelihoods, and people are likely to be more guarded about their privacy. There is no active monitoring of this area that I can detect. If I am to take something, I simply need to go about it calmly so as not to disturb people's suspicions. I have yet to see any security patrolling or cameras monitoring here inside, which leads me to believe that they would not check the restrooms for anything out of the ordinary. As I enter the restroom, I notice a plastic card on the ground near a stall. I pick it up and see that the words Quantum Communications Technical Support are scrawled in fancy letters across the back, while the front has the likeness of a young male along with his name and position. I place the card in my pocket and exit the restroom to continue my search of the building.

If I could wait until the building is a little more deserted, I can break into one of the suites with computers and make off with some high-dollar equipment. After closing, it is apparent that a couple of suites are left unsecured, with door locks disengaged. As I make a tour of the third floor, it becomes apparent that some type of telecommunications business takes up the entire floor. I notice a sign on one of the many doors, pull the card I found in the restroom out, and hold it up to the door. Both sign and card read Technical Support.

Returning to his law-abiding train of thought, our manager finds himself on the third floor in something of a daze, having been mentally immersed in his role-playing. Other scenarios rush through his mind as he urgently walks back to his office, where he will place a call to the local police department to follow up on his data request. More determined than ever to complete the crime analysis, our manager is thankful that he decided to look into the security and well-being of his property.

6

Methodology

In the sciences, theory and rote memorization are not sufficient to achieve significant scientific advances, or to lead mankind further into its development. Likewise, crime analysis principles must be applied to progress toward effective crime prevention. It is with this understanding and the knowledge gained thus far, that the methodology or process of crime analysis can be examined.

What is process and what makes it such a pivotal issue not only in discussions of crime analysis, but also in all walks of life? Process is what holds all disciplines together. An in-depth understanding, respect, and devotion to it are imperative in penetrating the armor of a discipline's mystique. Process can be defined simply as how an act is accomplished, and that can be expanded to include the development of additional techniques in the most effective and efficient fashion. Truly, one can use such a fundamental paradigm as spiritual belief to illustrate process in a belief's observance and its continual growth and progression through the centuries. Without process, there is chaos and disorder; with it one finds that tasks are ultimately more fulfilling. It is the method in the madness.

Using the example of teaching mathematics to a child, new teachers are trained to effectively communicate crucial points as well as the bridges between each detail to create a holistic understanding. Learning is hindered when concepts are presented as isolated components with little relation to dependent conceptual fixtures, but when one considers the additional task of coalescing modular elements, both the teacher and student may lose track of the object lesson as well as the process. By keeping the Gestalt of the task within sight, the student has a more fulfilled experience. In mathematics, the importance of showing one's work cannot be over-emphasized because close examination of the logic between problem and solution will reveal where errors or transpositions occurred, in essence, where process strayed. From there, errors can be rectified within the problem and subsequent errors can be prevented from building on previous ones.

Process is especially important within crime analysis since it requires that certain steps be reached and built on before fruitful security and crime prevention programs can be accomplished. One simply does not arrive at conclusions by taking a quick glance at raw data, but rather by careful separation of statistics into meaningful arrays where they can be easily consulted for comparison and cross-referencing. One must remember that crime analysis considers the past in order to help identify what will be targeted in the future, a crime archaeology of sorts where careful attention must be paid to each step of the process. When crime statistics are systemically studied, one creates an empirically sound methodology, which ultimately leads one to truth.

After the pertinent data (CFS and in-house security reports) for the given property or properties have been compiled, it must be coded to match the Federal Bureau of Investigation's (FBI) Uniform Crime Report (UCR) codification system, a rather simple process of changing crimes into numeric representations based on the crime's specific elements. Once accomplished, one can sort the property's activity by crime type and frequency, and then expand the scope to include temporal (time, day, date) and spatial (precise location) elements. As the work of arranging data arrays is completed, the information lends itself to graphical enhancements for easier comprehension. From there, the property's crime rates can be compared to that of other properties and to the city, state, and nation, and finally an appropriate defense may be constructed.

Arranging the information in the analysis for presentation purposes may take on many forms and can be accomplished as creatively or mundanely as one desires or requires. There are no absolutes regarding crime analysis formatting, though one would certainly want to convey the information clearly so interested parties (upper management, property owners, juries) will fully grasp the concept and the findings. Property managers and security service providers, like any other business entities, are often called on to present the results of new programs and should develop their presentation skills along with crime analysis skills to ensure funding for a long-term, successful crime prevention program.

The crime analysis format should be versatile and expandable so when new data become available or when management's needs change, different types of analysis may be added. One can imagine the re-formatting dilemma for every subsequent analysis if a suitable format is not developed at inception. Formatting ideas may be gleaned from our fictitious manager's own crime analysis discussed later.

One formatting alternative is of the computerized variety, specifically spreadsheet software that allows for organized data entry, complex calculations, color graphics, and, most importantly, the ability to be built on annually or as often as needed. Computer-based crime analysis avoids mountains of paper to sort through, and even in printed format, spreadsheet-derived data make for appealing professional presentations. One drawback realized in using computers and spreadsheet software is that unless computers and software are already a part of the management operation, they are expensive to obtain. It does take at least a cursory knowledge of a software application's capability. Analysts will find solace in that the software needed is not specific to crime analysis, and in most cases, common office applications such as Microsoft Excel, Word, PowerPoint, Lotus 123, Harvard Graphics, and WordPerfect can be utilized effectively.

In contrast to the streamlined approach of computer-aided work, the same analysis can be rendered with the old standby pencil and paper, which is welcome news to those uncomfortable with computers or who feel greater connections to tasks when they flow directly from the hands. Everyone learns differently, and perhaps the most important aspect of any discipline is its understanding and the ability to maintain a dynamic enthusiasm and learning curve. Conventional pencil and paper analysis has its drawbacks in that it is visually limiting in final presentation as well as time consuming, but there is no "According to Hoyle" set of rules behind crime analysis formatting, and the individual should exploit whatever means necessary to capture the activity's essence.

Once the data, including CFS, offense reports, and in-house security reports for the property have been assembled, it needs to be translated into a standardized set of codes that denote actual crimes. To ease comparisons, the UCR codification system should be used as it is simplistic and other data sets already use it. If anything other than UCR codes is provided, then the crimes must be transferred to UCR codes. This is required because police reports may differ in how they are worded or coded from the norm or from one another. To simplify matters the UCR coding system is recommended as it includes a fairly complete listing of possible crimes, which will make analysis that much more complete. A listing of the UCR coding system is as follows:

1. Murder
2. Rape
3. Robbery
4. Aggravated Assault
5. Burglary
6. Theft
7. Motor Vehicle Theft
8. Arson
9. Other Assaults
10. Forgery and Counterfeiting
11. Fraud
12. Embezzlement
13. Stolen Property—Buying, Receiving, Possessing
14. Vandalism

15. Weapons—Carrying, Possessing, etc.
16. Prostitution and Commercialized Vice
17. Sex Offenses
18. Drug Abuse Violations
19. Gambling
20. Offenses Against the Family and Children
21. Driving Under the Influence
22. Liquor Laws
23. Drunkenness
24. Disorderly Conduct
25. Vagrancy
26. All other offenses
27. Suspicion
28. Curfew and Loitering Laws (persons under 18)
29. Runaways (persons under 18)

Several different types of analysis make up a crime analysis as a whole. These would include crime-specific analysis, property-specific analysis, spatial analysis, and temporal analysis. Each of these modes of analysis examine an aspect of crime's impact on a property, when a crime is committed, where on the property it was committed, what crime was committed, and indirectly what measures are appropriate to counter such threats.

CRIME-SPECIFIC ANALYSIS

Crime-specific analysis focuses on the type of crimes committed on the property, endeavoring to enumerate the amount of crimes such as murder, rape, robbery, aggravated assault, and other crimes. This will aid management in knowing the specific type of problem, to what degree it exists, and indirectly what specific prevention measures can be used to reign in those problems if not eradicate them completely. Another benefit of this type of analysis is that a breakdown by crime will help to indicate a violent or property crime, what particular asset is being targeted and the resulting loss or damage to that particular target, and the implications of that loss or damage. As already mentioned, this data should be coded in compliance to the FBI's Uniform Crime Report system for ease of comparison among properties and to a lend a universality to the data if one should ever have the opportunity to compare one's analysis to a property managed by a colleague who has done the same. In transferring CFS or written descriptions, available offense reports and in-house security reports can come in handy for the purposes of confirmation as some written descriptions can be ambiguous at best. With practice, the analyst will be able to spot such discrepancies and become acquainted with the sub-process of verifying crimes.

PROPERTY-SPECIFIC ANALYSIS

What is high crime? What is low crime? Crime rate comparison is the best method for understanding crime levels on a given property, and as one determines the property's crime rate, comparisons are easily made against other properties under management's control, similar businesses in the area, and other geographic levels (census tract, police beat, city, MSA, state, and nation). For these and resource allocation reasons, crime analysis should be focused at the property level.

TEMPORAL ANALYSIS

In efficiently allocating crime prevention resources, crime analysis should include temporal details of a property's crime. Various methods for learning a property's crime patterns can be considered, including time of day, days of week, week of the month, seasonal trends, and, on the extreme, crime trends during full moons. Hindsight being 20–20, when past crimes can be identified by their proverbial fingerprints, the question of when can be answered. If there is evidence that particular crimes occur during certain periods, management can focus additional efforts on defending against crime during those time periods through deployment of security resources. Such considerations can save management money, and any overall savings will be viewed as a return on investment in annual profit and loss statements.

SPATIAL ANALYSIS

Spatial analysis brings a finer focus to the crime dilemma and leads to a holistic crime picture. Still, the principle of past activity shining the light of where attention is needed proves to be both necessary and advantageous to management, and is again applicable to this mode of analysis. Spatial analysis concerns itself with specific targets within the property and the lines of defense violated to get to the targets. To use our running example, such areas as the parking garage, common areas, areas surrounding the entrances and exits, as well as the individual suites inside exemplify targets where spatial analysis works to sharpen our focus by demanding answers to questions such as: Specifically where does the problem stem from? Through what door did an intruder enter the property? At what point did an attack take place between the building exit and the parking garage? Around what certain corner was an attacker hiding before perpetrating the crime?

Knowing the answers to these questions can help in determining the nature of defenses that are at our disposal as well as where and where not to concentrate our specific efforts. For example, if our manager realizes that the parking garage is the paramount source of crime, emphasizing security for the suites inside the building would certainly do little to arrest the rather obvious problem at hand. In summation, a spatial analysis can help bring problem areas to light, whereas the areas might be given to obscurity. One can think of spatial analysis as the compass rose in the map to crime prevention.

MODUS OPERANDI (MO) ANALYSIS

Modus Operandi (MO) analysis seeks to learn the criminal method of operation and answers the how question. Dependent on the availability of details culled from in-house security reports, offense reports, or interviews with victims, witnesses, and offenders, MO analysis determines an offender's criminal tactics that separate their crimes from other criminals. MO information is sometimes difficult to come by, but management can mandate that the property's staff maintains detailed reports of all activity (criminal or otherwise). Using temporal, spatial, and MO analysis, one will know more about the property's criminal nature, and a better defense can be created.

From the analysis, certain occurrences will make themselves known. Some crimes such as mugging (robbery) on days when people are to be paid from their jobs might make sense when one considers what has been learned about rational choice theory and routine activity, or that home burglaries tend to occur when the home is unattended, or that shoplifting tends to occur more frequently when a business is sparsely staffed. If such a fact in a given area is known and known enough by criminals, then the seed of criminal activity can be planted and come to fruition when such times arrive. Such occurrences happen for a reason. Combating the criminal mind is not the same as fighting a completely random opponent, but rather that certain tendencies stem from reasons culminating from a sort of benefit-loss analysis on the criminal's behalf mercifully tips the law-abiding public off from time to time as to what may be coming at them. When information such as this is present, one should take full advantage. Like much in crime analysis, proficiency in this area comes with practice and subsequent study on the subject, but one must agree that the analysis will become more meaningful as such skills are developed and additional knowledge is accrued.

Another benefit that pattern analysis produces is the highlighting of hot spots or places where crime has struck frequently enough to be deemed predictable. It has been found that certain places tend to stand out as havens for crime. Factors contributing to such labels may be as innocuous as random error, changes in an area's law-abiding and responsible population, decreases in the standard of living or increases in transient population, as well as less than innocent circumstances such as a particularly unfortunate chain of crimes. When a preponderance of crime impacts an area, one considers crime in that area to be clustered. Such properties that tend to experience a disproportionate amount of predatory crime tend to be accessible, contain or exhibit belongings or goods that are appealing to criminals, and to the criminal mind, show little promise of resistance to criminal acts. A clustered area can be easier to defend simply from the standpoint that the criminal acts are not clandestine, but tend to be brazenly committed because crime is so prevalent that an area has a dangerous reputation. Authorities as well as citizens may be either too busy thwarting the abundance of crime or are outmanned to the extent that a situation is out of control. Hard work will be needed to correct the problem, as well as careful supervision, revision, and at times complete upheaval of a system that is ineffective and the implementation of stronger measures.

Crime rates, like most statistics, exist to actively represent events that transpired or to extend that number to forecast future occurrences. Within crime analysis, crime rates assess a property's risk of violent and property crime victimization. The calculation of crime rates is fairly uncomplicated and requires little more than two pieces of data, one is a management-derived figure and the other is gleaned from the crime analysis. Simply stated, the violent crime rate is calculated by dividing the number of crimes by the traffic level and then multiplying by 1,000, the number commonly used to compare crime rates across the various levels of geographic analysis. Property crime rates, on the other hand, use the number of property targets as the denominator.

For example, burglary rates are calculated by dividing the number of burglary events by the number of targets. In a large apartment community with 2,000 units and 5,000 residents, the appropriate denominator for calculating the property crime rate is 2,000, while the denominator for calculating the violent crime rate is 5,000. Taking this example further, if the community experienced 25 violent crimes and 200 property crimes during the preceding year, the violent crime rate is 0.005 [(25/5,000) × 1,000], while the property crime rate is 100 [(200/2,000) × 1,000]. Simply stated, for crimes against persons, the denominator should be the number of persons. For crimes against properties, the denominator should be the number of properties.

While what has been discussed in this chapter has been largely geared toward flat, one-dimensional numbers, it is important to discuss alternatives to data presentation. As mentioned earlier, spreadsheets tend to make the material more presentable than pencil and paper calculations, but people learn on different levels, and the analyst should prepare the information for presentation in graphical form. As the axiom borrowed for this section's title suggests, graphical representation adds another dimension to synthesized data and might enable those who would remain unconvinced of situations at hand to see clearly the true course the property is headed.

APPLICATION

As our manager has just received the final piece of the puzzle in the form of CFS from the local police department, he reviews his schedule for the following week and pencils in a four-hour block on Wednesday morning to review the data. In the meantime, he retrieves all the crime information he has compiled over the last couple of weeks from his files and sets it on a table next to his computer.

As Wednesday morning arrives, our manager's anticipation has grown, and he is eager to sow the fruit of his labor and ascertain the criminal makeup of his building. In his hands, he now has all the raw data needed to conduct the crime analysis: CFS for the building property obtained from the local police department; the patrol beat statistics for the entire city, also obtained from the local police department; and finally, five books comprising a series called *Crime in the United States*, each representing individual years acquired from the FBI's Uniform Crime Report Division.

Our manager has weighed the advantages and disadvantages of a paper and pencil method of crime analysis versus a computer-assisted spreadsheet and selects the latter for its ability to easily calculate crime rates, create graphics, identify crime patterns and trends, and cross-reference criminal and other events. He begins by opening a box filled with perforated sheets listing all the crimes reported from his building during the past five calendar years. On the top of the stack is a code list to help him convert the CFS codes to UCR codes so he may make fair comparisons to other properties, and the city and state.

He begins entering each CFS into the crime database. It is from this database that our manager will verify the crimes and perform the various analyses to determine when and where crime prevention measures are needed, as well as what type of measure will be most appropriate. The process of entering data is fairly simplistic and takes him only an hour to complete. From this point, he will re-code the data to match that of the UCR.

THE CODING PROCESS

Optimally, one would like to create a master list from the CFS that shares the UCR coding system and will be the source of subsequent analysis. From what he has learned, our manager knows that the coding process may include one, two, or three steps dependent on the type of CFS system that his local police department utilizes. He begins by comparing the UCR codes he received from the FBI to that of the codes from those used by the local police department as outlined on the code sheets he was provided. They do not match. Thus, he knows that he has found himself in the midst of a three-step process. Table 6–1 is one sheet from the many he received from the police department.

First, using the CFS code sheets provided by the police department, he re-labels the CFS codes into the actual crimes that the codes represent. For example, all 63 codes are labeled theft, 4 are labeled aggravated assault, 83 are labeled burglary, etc. Once he has labeled all the crimes, he sets out to convert the names of crime in their equivalent UCR code. All thefts are coded 6, all burglaries are coded

Table 6–1 Police Calls for Service, 4406 Young Street.

Run 03/15/00 by Officer SK Jones

Incident Number	Dispatch Date	Report Time	PDC	Incident
991478	010299	1635	83	Burglary
991499	010399	2205	121	Fight in Progress
991512	010599	1950	63	Theft
991551	010699	1407	4	Aggravated Assault
991568	010799	1632	63	Theft
991585	010999	0959	17	Robbery in Progress
991602	011199	0843	14	Sexual Assault
991619	011399	1745	4	Aggravated Assault
991636	011599	1552	83	Burglary
991653	011699	0711	63	Theft
991670	011799	1607	83	Burglary
991687	011899	0156	83	Burglary
991704	012099	1337	63	Theft
991721	012199	1222	14	Sexual Assault
991738	012299	2207	83	Burglary
991755	012499	1033	15	Auto Theft
991772	012599	1153	83	Burglary
991789	012699	1514	15	Auto Theft
991806	012899	1050	121	Fight in Progress
991823	012999	1521	14	Sexual Assault

5, and aggravated assaults are coded 4, etc. Once he has re-coded all the crimes to UCR, he notes that there are 260 incidents in total in his list, each represents an index crime reported from his property. For each of the 260 entries, he creates a row in the spreadsheet for each factor gleaned from the CFS: incident number, date the incident was reported, and time the incident was reported, and then using a calendar, he adds a column denoting the day of week that each incident was reported. Table 6–2 shows the first 20 entries of his work in date order.

Looking back at his spreadsheets, our manager feels it would be prudent to reconcile the data with the original CFS sheets to

Table 6–2

Date Reported	Day of Week	Time Reported	UCR Code	UCR Description
02-Jan-99	Saturday	4:35 p.m.	5	Burglary
03-Jan-99	Sunday	10:05 p.m.	9	Other Assault (Fight)
05-Jan-99	Tuesday	7:50 p.m.	6	Theft
06-Jan-99	Wednesday	2:07 p.m.	4	Aggravated Assault
07-Jan-99	Thursday	4:32 p.m.	6	Theft
09-Jan-99	Saturday	9:59 a.m.	3	Robbery
11-Jan-99	Monday	8:43 a.m.	2	Rape
13-Jan-99	Wednesday	5:45 p.m.	4	Aggravated Assault
15-Jan-99	Friday	3:52 p.m.	5	Burglary
16-Jan-99	Saturday	7:11 a.m.	6	Theft
17-Jan-99	Sunday	4:07 p.m.	5	Burglary
18-Jan-99	Monday	1:56 a.m.	5	Burglary
20-Jan-99	Wednesday	1:37 p.m.	6	Theft
21-Jan-99	Thursday	12:22 p.m.	2	Rape
22-Jan-99	Friday	10:07 p.m.	5	Burglary
24-Jan-99	Sunday	10:33 a.m.	7	Auto Theft
25-Jan-99	Monday	11:53 a.m.	5	Burglary
26-Jan-99	Tuesday	3:14 p.m.	7	Auto Theft
28-Jan-99	Thursday	10:50 a.m.	9	Other Assault (Fight)
29-Jan-99	Friday	3:21 p.m.	2	Rape

ensure that there have been no mistakes in data entry. Finding no errors in his work, he prints a copy of what he has created thus far and sends it with a cover letter to the local police department requesting the public information section of the offense/incident reports for each incident listed.

PATTERNS AND TRENDS

Our manager decides to map out each event in expanded fashion, so if he should want to trace a specific week or month, and cross-reference trends found there with extemporaneous factors that may have influenced the crimes. To facilitate this activity, our manager

Table 6–3

JANUARY 1999	FEBRUARY 1999	MARCH 1999
Burglary	Auto Theft	Theft
Other Assault (Fight)	Theft	Theft
Theft	Theft	Theft
Aggravated Assault	Aggravated Assault	Other Assault (Fight)
Theft	Burglary	Auto Theft
Robbery	Theft	Other Assault (Fight)
Rape	Burglary	Burglary
Aggravated Assault	Burglary	Theft
Burglary	Theft	Theft
Theft	Theft	Auto Theft
Burglary	Other Assault (Fight)	Theft
Burglary	Robbery	Theft
Theft	Theft	Auto Theft
Rape	Burglary	
Burglary	Theft	
Auto Theft	Theft	
Burglary		
Auto Theft		
Other Assault (Fight)		
Rape		

makes a calendar for each year covered in the analysis and notes the crimes by month and year until all five years are completed. Table 6–3 shows the first three months.

In looking at a portion of the calendar he has produced in the computer spreadsheet, note that he has taken each incident from the master list and placed it in an empty spot (cell) corresponding with the appropriate month and year of when the incident was reported. For more compact analysis, calendars can prove to be somewhat cumbersome, so for tighter uses, our manager compiles a series of tables that will allow him to spot trends and patterns. First, our manager sets out to total each crime to determine the frequency at which crimes are occurring at his building during the year (see Table 6–4).

Table 6–4 Frequency of Index Crimes.

Crime	Subtotal	Percentage
Murder	1	0
Rape	3	1
Robbery	6	2
Aggravated Assault	8	3
Burglary	21	8
Theft	145	56
Auto Theft	76	29
Arson	0	0
Total	260	100

Table 6–5 Frequency of Crime by Year.

Year	Subtotal	Percentage
1995	117	13
1996	138	15
1997	172	19
1998	221	24
1999	260	29
Total	908	100

As seen in his frequency table, note that he has simply totaled the number of each crime reported and totaled them back to the original number of entries of 260, ensuring that he has not over- or undercounted any crime. He then sets out to determine if a crime trend exists on an annual basis for the years he has included in his analysis. In doing so, he creates Table 6–5 for the past five years. Our manager's table shows a clear upward crime trend beginning in 1995 and carrying on through 1999. It is important from time to time to make certain that the mathematical aspect of an analysis is correct. While computers can make analysis easier, computers can do only what users instruct them to do, and if the commands issued are faulty, then the fruit of computer operations will act as an opportunity to catch any mistakes in data entry. As mentioned earlier in the chapter, attention to detail is crucial for accurate analysis, so it is advisable to take a moment now and again to check one's work for such errors.

Table 6–6 represents the Frequency of Crime by Quarter. This bit of analytical detailing reveals that crime takes a strong upturn during the latter summer months (Quarter III) and fall and early winter months (Quarter IV). In ensuring the accuracy of his calculations, note that the total remains 260.

As seen in Table 6–7, note that our manager is trying to ascertain what day or days of the week pose the most threat to persons and property at his building. The results point toward a marked increase on Wednesdays, Thursdays, and Fridays, and that the relatively low crime on Saturday and Sunday can be attributed to the fact that most offices are closed on the weekend. Lastly, one can see that his total of 260 is consistent with the master list and his other tables.

Finally, in Table 6–8, he has created a breakdown of the crimes into four-hour blocks. As his table indicates, a significant majority of crime was reported between the hours of 12 p.m. and 7:59 p.m., with most reported between 4 p.m. and 7:59 p.m. Here again, note

Table 6–6 Frequency of Crime by Quarter.

Quarter	Sub-Total	Percentage
I	58	22
II	44	17
III	83	32
IV	75	29
Total	260	100

Table 6–7   Frequency of Crime by Day.

Day	Subtotal	Percentage
Sunday	17	7
Monday	37	14
Tuesday	36	14
Wednesday	44	17
Thursday	51	20
Friday	51	20
Saturday	24	9
Total	260	100

Table 6–8   Frequency of Crime by Time Period.

Time Period	Subtotal	Percentage
0000–0359	4	2
0400–0759	19	7
0800–1159	18	7
1200–1559	83	32
1600–1959	105	40
2000–2359	31	12
Total	260	100

that his total is 260, confirming that he has not made any mathematical errors in the process of creating his table.

Once he completed this first round of analysis, our manager prints out each table, spreads them out on his desk, and begins making a list of generalizations about the nature of crime on his property and his thoughts about each fact.

1. Theft is by far the most frequent problem at my building. However, the violent crimes pose a more serious threat to the people at the building and to the building's financial stability.

2. Crime in general has steadily increased since 1995. What is it about my building that allows for 260 violations? Have criminals known all along about the vulnerabilities that I discovered during my recent assessments of the building's security?
3. Crime occurs more frequently during quarters 3 and 4. Why are violations on my property occurring more frequently during the summer? Is it because kids are out of school and some are committing the thefts?
4. Crime tends to ebb and flow throughout the week, reaching its peak on Wednesdays, Thursdays, and Fridays before declining considerably on the weekends and leveling off for the first two workdays in the week. Maybe the criminals know that people usually get paid at the end of the week and that is when they are choosing to strike.
5. Crime is reported most frequently between 4 p.m. to 8 p.m., followed closely by the hours of noon to 4 p.m. I suppose that crime in general increases after darkness conceals illegal activities. The increase at 4 o'clock may be attributed to kids cutting through the parking garage and stealing from cars.

All of the analysis he has completed thus far has related strictly to his property, and though he has abundant information from that alone, he now wants to get a feel for his property as it relates, or compares, to his city and state. For this comparison, he gathers the violent crime totals for the city and state from the five books he received from the FBI for the relevant years of 1995 through 1999, as well as the population levels for these geographic areas for the same years. At last, he has all the external pieces of data he needs to calculate crime rates; however, he is lacking one figure—the population of the building. The population of a property is commonly known as the traffic level and usually includes employees, visitors, tenants, vendors, and any other people that may have reason to enter the premises. With these characteristics in mind, he determines the population of his building to be about 3,000 on any given day. Our manager writes out the violent crime rate formula he learned earlier on a scratch pad so he can input the correct numbers.

Violent Crime Rate (VCR)
= (Total Violent Crime/Population) × 1,000

And so he begins his calculations.
The building's VCR is

$$18/3,000 = .006$$

$$.006 \times 1,000 = 6.0$$

The building's VCR during the past year was 6.0.

Using his CFS and the FBI's *Crime in the United States*, our manager continues his calculations for each prior year and geographic level of analysis until he comes up with Table 6–9.

From this table, it becomes evident that at one time his property's violent crime rate was significantly lower on a per capita basis when compared to the city and state, yet recent years have proven that his property has suffered from a crime upswing. To fully understand the implications, our manager prepares a graph to visually depict the crime rate trends between 1995 and 1999. (See Figure 6–1.)

Finally, using the patrol beat statistics obtained from the local police department, our manager compares the crime in his patrol beat, A213, to the patrol beat average that he obtained by totaling the individual crimes for all patrol beats and dividing by number of beats in the city. Here, he remembers that the calculation of crime rates for the beat are not possible because the city does not collect population counts by patrol beat, and even if it did, surely the citizens of the city do not work in the same beat in which they live,

Table 6–9

	1995	1996	1997	1998	1999
Building	1.33	2.00	3.33	4.00	6.00
City	13.88	16.00	14.65	14.54	13.07
State	7.61	8.40	8.06	7.62	7.07

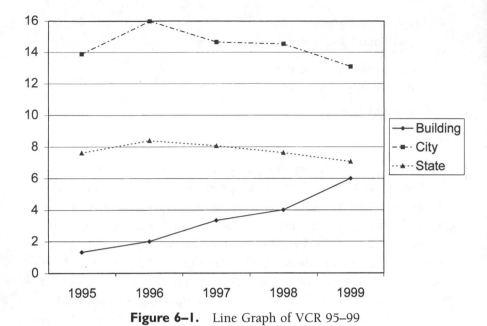

Figure 6–1. Line Graph of VCR 95–99

Table 6–10

	Total Violent Crime	Total Property Crime	Total Index Crime
1995 Beat Average	223.2	1,601.6	1,824.8
1995 Beat A213	242	2,358	2,600
1996 Beat Average	261.2	1,507.3	1,768.4
1996 Beat A213	319	1,925	2,244
1997 Beat Average	243.5	1,205.2	1,448.7
1997 Beat A213	245	1,737	1,982
1998 Beat Average	245.8	1,139.7	1,385.5
1998 Beat A213	309	1,837	2,146
1999 Beat Average	222.1	1,025.1	1,247.2
1999 Beat A213	290	1,719	2,009

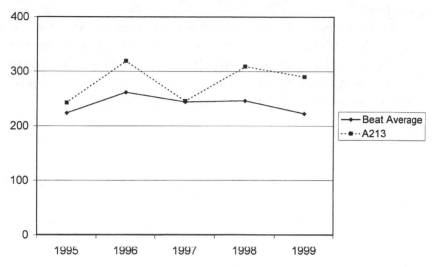

Figure 6–2. Beat VCL Graphic

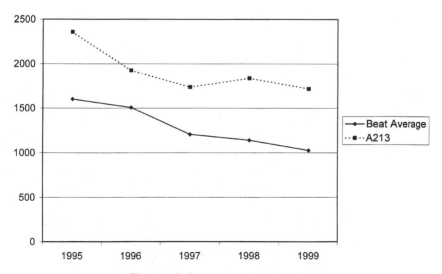

Figure 6–3. Beat PCL Graphic

rendering beat populations fluid during the course of a day. (See Table 6–10.)

From his patrol beat comparison chart, one can see that our manager has a bit of good news. Crime in beat A213, where the building is located, fluctuated only slightly above the average patrol beat during the years he has considered and on the whole is a relatively normal patrol beat. (See Figures 6–2 and 6–3.)

7

Crime Prevention Programs

In the game of American football, two schools of thought have had a notable impact on our current vernacular and have made their way into collective American thought: The best defense is a good offense and, conversely, the best offense is a good defense. To a large extent, the American military borrowed the former as its strategic framework during the 1980s as it stockpiled nuclear weapons and consistently pushed the ends of the technological envelope, which as history shows played a prominent role in bringing the Cold War to a peaceful conclusion. When the circumstances and resources allow, this strategy works extremely well despite its headstrong premise. For crime analysis, and more specifically, crime prevention, the latter serves well as food for thought as one examines some of the ideas that have been gathered through the years regarding the practical prevention of crime on the property.

Some may think of prevention as a passive action in that without focus on the apprehension and punishment of criminals, the remaining options are that of victims trying all their worth to prevent such an occurrence of crime from happening to them again. Crime prevention does not operate on the pretense that turning back time and preventing the crime in that manner is a viable option, but instead it remains within logical boundaries and works with very real limitations given by budget, overall feasibility, and knowledge of past crimes. Dealing with the relative reactivity of prevention over apprehension, this perception is true only when looking at the short-term scenario. When examining the long-term effects of both types of philosophies, however, logic should prove that criminals cannot commit as many crimes if the arenas in which they have run rampant in the past will in the future make their exploits unwelcome, if not impossible. By weakening and eventually tearing down a criminal's opportunity structure for crime, the criminal will have to look elsewhere to commit crimes. One historical parallel would be the stratagem used by the Russians in 1812 when, to thwart an attacking Napoleon, they burned the city of Moscow. This saved the humiliation of the city's capture and left Napoleon and his forces stalled in Russia facing formidable conditions brought on by a brutal winter.

Quality crime prevention seeks to recognize the nature of crime and to some extent use its own momentum against it. This type of prevention might resemble a Zen approach in that efficiency and the expansion of seemingly innocuous processes are sought. If a crime cannot be prevented, then at least the vulnerability of a property should be limited to restrict damage and/or loss. Prevention should examine the ways a property is vulnerable and design the security around those areas of weakness. A fine example of this can be found in the change of compact disc packaging. A newer, smaller, and more expensive product, it did not take disc retailers long to find that significant losses were being incurred from their rather untraceable exodus. Deconstructing the problem, it was found that being thin and square in shape, the discs could be slipped underneath clothing or into shopping bags without detection or arousing the suspicions of most store personnel who did not witness the actual theft. The answer, a deterrent: A long, rectangular box hollowed out at the top to house the actual compact disc. A would-be thief would have a tougher time stealing and concealing a stolen compact disc, and even if they could, the increased size of the packaging made multiple theft that much more difficult. This appeared to solve the problem for a time until it was found that thieves were ripping the discs straight out of the long boxes and once again were making off with the small, squared discs. Granted, this required a more intricate, two-step action to complete the theft, but still, a breach occurred. Acting according to the nature of the problem, distributors instituted another prevention plan, which was to affix a sensor tag onto the plastic wrap covering the exterior of the disc, which would trigger an alarm typically at the front of the retail outlet. The beauty of this system is that employees must scan each individual disc to clear the alarm. To date, this system has proven to be the best means of prevention for the given merchandise. As one can see, this was the result of a trial-and-error process, but each progressive step brought marked improvement.

BUSINESS AND CRIME PREVENTION

In considering Chapter 1, remember how our manager felt toward crime. He was apathetic to crime and was unaware of its unfavorable effect on his property, his tenants, and their customers. From his perspective and doubtless the perspective shared by many property managers across the United States: It has nothing to do with my business. Crime is not a real threat to my business or me. Crime is much lower than what people say. Judging by the truth—that crime is a real threat and does occur far more frequently than should be acceptable—one would be inclined to think that quite a few property managers do feel the way that our manager once felt or at the very least are seemingly oblivious to crime's possibility. Increasingly, business is concerned with production and with cold numbers symbolic of performance levels. There is little choice in business to remain idle for any length of time, as just about every competitor in any given industry is out to exploit any advantage given. This is the mindset in which most business is conducted, a contentious environment, if you will. If business is warfare, then crime is a field of land mines— you cannot see them and may even take for granted their presence, but when they explode, you fear them.

Rectifying the problem, getting around the obstacle as it were, requires first that the impact of crime on the property be acknowledged and not merely for the reason that it is a nuisance and another ink blot on the appointment book, but because it is sound business practice.

Our skeptical friends in business may furrow a brow at the proposed notion, but sound crime prevention can eliminate unnecessary costs such as increased insurance premiums and jury awards for actual and punitive damages incurred should a crime on the property result in injury or loss. Other benefits include security costs that will be allocated toward measures more proactive than reactive, dealing with future crime rather than past crimes, as well as a marked increase in employee morale, attendance, and overall productivity. Simply put, how much does the employer care about the little person in the operation? Answers to this question may directly lead to answers as to why employee turnover spirals out of control and begs the question, Are employees more than just numbers on a page? If care does not imply security then what does? And how is an existing or potential client supposed to view such carelessness? Another consideration is that one customer or employee with disappointing news to report on a company's behalf (even if the company itself is not directly charged with property security, it has entrusted it to a less than responsible party and therefore is ultimately at fault) can set off a separate tangent of second-hand criticism whose impact can be both far-reaching and detrimental. It would be unfortunate enough if a company had to dole out additional training costs for new employees, but what if those new employees were less than forthcoming due to a wounded corporate image? If it is true that the serious business community will think only about crime as it relates directly to profit and loss, then an interested or skeptical individual might want to inquire into obtaining some average actual and punitive settlements, factor those into the overall costs, and then visualize those costs partially absorbed by preventive measures.

CRIME PREVENTION PROCESS

As in the previous chapter where process was key, the same holds true in implementing and maintaining a successful crime prevention program. The first step in such a process is to have completed a crime analysis as described throughout this volume, and from that effort gathered a knowledge of crime's nature, the number of crimes, how and when they are being committed, and where the breach lies in the previous defense. This, in turn, prepares for selecting the measures of security one will apply to the situation. There are a variety of factors to consider that will be touched on in this section, so when making a selection, one can choose those measures that will be both effective and efficient as possible, given obvious financial constraints as well as other limitations to making one's property a fortress. An individual should think of these preventive measures as a newly constructed roof and subsequent crime as the storm he or she strives to keep from soaking the interior. There are no legal guidelines for how closely one should monitor crime; that knowledge comes from experience and industry standards. With the prevention process in mind, attention turns to the degree at which defenses might operate, given the severity of potential crimes.

The highest level of defense is a stand against crime that makes the following statement: Zero tolerance. Risk Avoidance can be thought of as denying the criminal situation by removing the target from the property altogether, hence making it completely inaccessible and eliminating all temptation. An example of this might be storing personal valuables off the property in a bank's locked vault or a safe deposit box where the valuables will not be affected by the property's crime situation or contributory environment.

When targets cannot be removed completely, a less intrusive intervention must be used. Risk Reduction strives to reduce threats to crime targets, while allowing the flow of day-to-day operations to continue without disruption. While trying to operate within the hazards of a cash-based business, the convenience store industry has developed a highly successful method of risk reduction. The use of time-lock safes that limit the amount of cash that can be removed at any one time has helped to reduce the number of crimes that affect convenience stores and decrease the gains made by criminals.

Our next entry on the hierarchy of defense is the concept of Risk Spreading, which involves the use of crime prevention measures to ensure protection at several stages of a criminal act. A target can be protected in such a way by physical barriers, such as a structure that has few points of entry, and those necessary are well attended to deny the perpetrator access to the property. If a person should make his or her way onto the property, measures are taken to detect and monitor the person's presence, which will help in delaying the offender, giving the authorities an opportunity to apprehend him or her. Such tactics may be employed through the use of fencing, the strategic placement of vegetation, monitored closed-circuit television, alarm systems, security personnel, and "No Trespassing" signs.

A more passive type of defense is Risk Transfer, usually accomplished with the purchase of insurance. In this scenario, the risk is moved into the domain of a third party who accepts it for a stipend. As with the previous echelons of defense, Risk Transfer may be the tonic for a certain situation that either cannot be properly protected or is such that its very nature seems to solicit and invite security risks, such as diamonds and other jewelry. Obviously such merchandise must be displayed in order to be effectively sold, but in doing so, there is inherent risk, and in a scenario such as this, a Risk Transfer may be necessary after the previous methods have been utilized to potential.

Much less of a defense and more of a realization is the notion of Risk Acceptance, wherein the business owner essentially assumes the risk of theft, loss, or damage into his or her operating costs. This may seem like a near capitulatory course of action, but if there is no other way to effectively protect one's investment, then perhaps through creative financing, a business owner may be able to depreciate the cost of the risk or pass it on to his or her customers. On the whole, Risk Acceptance is essentially relying on fate that the property will remain unharmed.

CRIME PREVENTION MEASURES

Three main categories exist for crime prevention measures. While they can be classified as such, no ascribed practice states that aspects of one category cannot be used in conjunction with aspects of other categories; in fact; if the sum effect is a positive one, it would be recommended.

The first security measure falls under the heading of policies and procedures. This type of security measure is the least expensive to design, implement, and maintain. This mostly written measure entails the composition and enforcement of guidelines to be carried out by security and non-security personnel, such as adhering to designated entry ways; the reporting of crimes, suspicious activity, shortages, and losses; as well as details seemingly innocuous as making certain that entrances are sealed before, during, and after business hours. Also to be considered are the necessities of keeping security measures focused, such as the maintenance of daily in-house reports, reports that account for extraordinary occurrences, and checklists to ensure that all areas of the property have been secured. As stated before, this area of prevention is the least costly, but nevertheless requires attention and updating to bring the guidelines up to speed in regard to the changing needs of the property. Another consideration is that the wording of policies should be flexible enough to provide for contingencies and change, but should not be so malleable that loopholes appear and allow policies to slacken, which can be a security risk itself.

Our next category involves the purchase and installation of physical security measures such as electronic surveillance devices, metal detectors, closed-circuit television, electronic entry card readers, and additional communications equipment to facilitate reported emergencies. In addition, lighting hardware, time-control devices, and hidden safes may be considered as prudent investments, given particular situations. These measures may tally great expense, and because of that expense, management should evaluate carefully the advantages and disadvantages based on the crime analysis before engaging in such purchase. Management should take into account that machinery breaks down and otherwise needs repair, and that timely maintenance should also be thought of as part of the cost. There is little doubt that such equipment can positively impact crime on the property provided that the chosen measures match the actual needs and budgetary constraints. One should not purchase every available (and they are numerous) gadget that claims to be a safe-guard against crime. Management should be especially prudent in such purchases, delving into what resources are available to conduct research on the effectiveness and efficiency of a device. Management should look for reputable brands and manufacturers who have a proven track record of producing worthwhile goods that are known not to be plagued with mechanical or design problems. Much of this goes without saying, but when considering today's marketplace and the wealth of merchandise offered, it is truly a tidbit of good advice that bears both repeating and heeding.

Finally, the third main category of security measures is personnel. Security personnel expand to include armed and non-armed security officers, armored car services, couriers, and guard dog handlers. A great deal of the prudence offered in regard to the previous category is applicable to this category as well. Management should stress reliability and proven results from all of the aforementioned security personnel.

Despite the obvious costs of security equipment, it should come as no surprise to find that security personnel is the most expensive of all three categories mentioned. This can be attributed to the fact that security personnel are paid by the hour and thus should be considered a fixed and recurring expense. Similarly, armored car services and couriers are paid by the occasion and may also fall under the heading of fixed expenses. Though its cost may be spread out over time, physical security equipment may be most expensive at the time it is acquired and installed. Management will find that security personnel will carry the greatest cost in terms of direct fees for their services, but also hold with them the danger of increased liability for false arrests, illegal searches and seizures, and possible injuries to customers, and even criminals. Regardless of the potential problems, one may find that for particular situations, a human presence is needed to supplement existing crime prevention policies, procedures, and physical measures to provide the property with adequate protection. Under these circumstances, the greatest crime prevention benefits may come from personnel who can react to myriad situations that may arise in a criminal incident. Security personnel can obviously react positively or negatively, but the best reactions will come with proper hiring, training, and supervision.

As mentioned many times over in this volume, crime should be examined as independently as possible from external factors while emphasizing the specific property, its problems, and its potential. In maintaining this line of thinking, Situational Crime Prevention involves forms of deterrence expressly designed to combat specific crimes with the use of exterior environmental forces in ways that inhibit crime by removing enabling factors.

One should draw their focus on property-specific crime reduction measures closer and examine particular techniques that an individual may find of use when fleshing out the sketches of a crime prevention program. The first emphasis is increasing real or perceived effort on the part of management in the effort to reduce crime or steer it elsewhere. Some might think of this aspect as a ploy, and granted some of the examples are less substantive than others, but let us remember that prior to the troop landings at Omaha Beach in the invasion of Europe on D-Day, a large part of that operation's success was due to the effective charade perpetrated by General George Patton situated in North Africa. The Axis powers, convinced of a mass build-up originating from North Africa coupled with their belief that Patton would definitely be the one to spearhead any attack of necessary magnitude to enter Europe, exposed a weakness that enabled Allied forces to pull off one of the most spectacular turnabouts in military, if not world, history. Though the techniques discussed in the text will prove to be more potent than Patton's faux infantry exercises and plastic blow-up tanks, the root of the plan is the same—controlling the perception of the opposition.

ACCESS CONTROL

The first technique sub-category is the concept of target hardening or the fortification of the property. Target hardening, generally speaking, involves the use of barriers, both tangible and intangible, such as equipping doors with locks and deadbolts, surrounding the property perimeter with fences, securing interior possessions in safes, and training in-house security employees in self-defense skills. Other related techniques would include using automobile prevention devices such as The Club and other types of steering wheel locks.

The next sub-category involves access control, the purpose of which is to limit the number of building entry risks through the use of physical and psychological barriers. Barriers are used to discourage attack. In the physical form, they form concentric circles around assets requiring protection. For example, to protect the revenues of a store located in a strip center, the money (including marked bills) is kept in a safe behind locked office doors of a locked store. The strip center is guarded by a security officer who is directed by policies and procedures in a parking lot that has controlled traffic flow and limited escape routes. Other specific examples of access control might be gates, security officer booths, in-house security personnel, Personal Identification Number (PIN) codes and identification badges, retinal-scanning devices, voice recognition systems, entry phones, and doormen. In addition, these measures can be used in conjunction with shrubbery, trees, and any other natural barrier already in place as they are excellent instruments in diverting attempted entry away from the property.

Another method to keep in mind is to deflect offenders from clients and employees. In doing this, management uses the principles of Routine Activity by preventing the mixing of offenders and targets to reduce the opportunity structure for crime. One can see examples of this in action when in crowded nightspots and other events where taxis, shuttles, and city buses are waiting to pick up patrons after closing time or when the event has ended. A situation that benefits from the avoidance of mixing targets and criminals is the closing of streets to vehicular traffic during street festivals and parades, giving pedestrians and potential victims a safe haven from vehicular traffic and urban predators prepared for a quick getaway while waiting in vehicles.

Finally, there is the idea of removing from the situation certain facilitators, which carry with them the potential to escalate encounters to violent and potentially lethal encounters. Throughout history, this technique has been used quite effectively to counter known threats. Look back to the Old West and a saloon owner's mandate that patrons check their firearms at the door, which for the most part subdued many a potential catastrophe into a comparatively innocuous fistfight. This is not to say that fists themselves cannot be lethal weapons, but in eliminating gun play from the mix, there is a greater opportunity for a hand-to-hand fight to be stopped or for the authorities to be called to the scene to intervene. Other parallels to this ideal include general gun control legislation, the limiting of alcohol consumption, automobiles outfitted with speed governors, and credit cards equipped with photo identification. This concept makes no pretensions that crime exists and occurs, but aims to figuratively and literally disarm what participants may choose to involve in a situation.

The next emphasis to be covered is something of a relation to the aforementioned group of techniques in that it deals with increasing perception, but also works to stress risks and consequences of crime mainly through authoritative presence and in some cases perception of presence. At the forefront of this concept is formal surveillance. Such a notion acts as a deterrent to offenders by maintaining the presence of security officers, police officers, and monitored closed-circuit television (CCTV). This can prove to be very costly to management, but in light of compelling crime reasons, costs may be justified. Personnel are usually able to immediately reduce occurrences in shoplifting or other similar theft and in any number of scenarios wherein physical altercations figure prominently. It should be remembered that the hiring of security personnel exposes management to criticisms not associated with other crime countermeasures, such as claims of illegal searches, false arrests, and negligent hiring, training, and supervision.

Screening

Less troublesome perhaps is the inclusion of entry/exit screening, which tends to ensure that those entering and exiting a property have a right to be on the premises and through basic visible search are not bringing contraband on the premises or leaving the property with stolen items. For example, some pawn shops screen customers via a visual check and a self-locking door, which the clerk must deactivate for the customer to be granted admission as well as when taking their leave of the premises. Other examples may include merchandise tags, baggage screening, metal detectors, metallic strips equipped with miniaturized sensors, and related electronic equipment. Of course, such measures can be costly, and without the proper degree of enforcement, maintenance, and support can be prone to loss and damage despite the efforts rendered.

Formal Surveillance

Similar to formal surveillance is observation conducted by employees. This technique occurs naturally as employees go about their normal duties and can be enhanced through crime prevention classes and documented in policies and procedures as well as training manuals. For natural guardianship to occur, high employee morale is a prerequisite. Employee surveillance is especially effective against internal theft in the retail industry when whistle-blower policies are well defined. Some specific techniques involving employee surveillance include valets watching over a parking lot as they wait for customers to arrive, stockers in grocery stores viewing the actions of customers as they go about their duties, and hotel maids finding illegal substances in a guest's room while cleaning. One obvious drawback to this concept is the fact that much of the effort behind it relies on the diligence of each employee and thereby depends on employee training, internalized company pride, work ethic, and an environment not characterized by a wholesale apathy on the part of those decidedly non-security professionals being charged with the additional responsibility.

Natural Surveillance

More matter of fact than anything else is the notion of natural surveillance, which involves the manipulation of the environment to allow for employees and consumers to enjoy high visibility of the common areas. This can be accomplished by ensuring that buildings contain many windows, ample lighting, low-cut shrubbery, and interior layouts that permit access and visibility to as many areas as is feasible. Once again, however, this technique is almost entirely dependent on the effort of non-security personnel and human nature. While the previous two techniques are not formal security measures, when used in concert with more proven modes of surveillance, the combination often proves to be just the sort of prevention program that both works cost effectively and does not encumber or hinder business operations.

Reducing Rewards

Along different lines, the crime prevention cause is enhanced by reducing anticipated rewards due the successful criminal act. The most obvious method of accomplishing this is by removing the target from the area of danger. As mentioned earlier, this is risk avoidance and is effective when instituted early on in the program design and for as many targets as feasible, while allowing daily business operations to endure. Borrowing a well-known phrase, this is akin to discretion being the better part of valor. There is certainly no glamour or excitement in avoidance, but oftentimes it is met with better results than its counterparts within the prevention continuum. Some examples of target removal include pay phones that use prepaid cards rather than coins, daily revenue deposits, safe deposit boxes, removable car stereos, women's shelters, and witness protection programs.

Property Identification

Similar to target removal, the identification of property is devoid of the more visceral aspects of prevention and protection, favoring a more cerebral approach that reduces criminal desire as illicit possession of a marked target would tend to enhance culpability and provide direct evidence of wrongdoing. Most can scan their homes, vehicles, and offices, and find an array of possessions that are marked for identification. While serial numbers and other identifying characteristics may aid in their eventual recovery should they be stolen, the chief aim of identification is to deter theft in the first place by expressing to offenders that the article in question can and will be recovered eventually and by virtue of identification renders resale difficult.

Denying Benefits

Related somewhat to property identification is the denying of benefits to offenders after the fact. That is, a sort of self-destruct contingency, which makes theft a moot option to the offender. This method attempts to render property useless if it is not obtained legitimately. It is used heavily in the retail clothing business to deter shoplifting by means of ink tags that release ink if tampered with, thus staining the clothes and rendering them useless. Other examples might be coded car radios, vehicle engine kill switches, and software registration numbers.

Reducing Temptation

Also included in this stream of thought is the reduction of offender temptation or the broken windows theory, whereby residents work to avoid neighborhood decay by fixing problems as they arise, which discourages criminal behavior and activity. As one remembers from Rational Behavior and Routine Activity, criminals choose their targets in relation to their probability of success and failure, risk, and reward. If an area is kept up to the point that a broken car window where a thief might enter the vehicle would be recognized immediately as being an out of the ordinary occurrence, then an offender may avoid the area for fear of being caught.

Removing Excuses

Lastly, there is the concept of removing excuses for criminal activity. Just as controlling facilitators in a situation may prevent the escalation of crimes to violent encounters, there are ways to control the amount and presence of less than obvious lapses in security. This technique applies more to a disruptive behavior by imposing a penalty or increasing the likelihood of detection and is exemplified by the following. We can close loopholes in the law (very common in revised IRS codes), hotels can require credit cards to hold reservations, hunters must wear their licenses in plain view, receipts for returns and exchanges can be required, and handicap parking permits must be displayed. Another way of removing excuses from the criminal acts is to stimulate the conscience of the given populace. This usually involves signage that potential offenders will read and follow such as "No Trespassing" signs, signs in a zoo stating not to feed or physically interact with the animals, signs in retail stores stating that shoplifters will be prosecuted, or unmonitored speed radar that displays a driver's speed.

Facilitating Compliance

Similarly, facilitating compliance can encourage conscience, making it that much easier for people, including offenders, to obey their better nature and the law. One can see how this works in the way that trashcans are provided to inspire litter-control consciousness, the amnesty periods for the return of library books, and the cessation of illegal cable service theft without fear of reprisals.

Discouraging Crime

Sometimes criminal activity can be inhibited by discouraging the act before it has manifested by appealing to psychological processes and attitudes that can cause crime. For example, Nazi Germany, by using propaganda, was able to sway otherwise ordinary lawful and moral citizens to agree with and perpetuate belief in concepts that enabled what is believed to be the most heinous of crimes against humanity to which this world has ever been witness. Like other approaches, this relies more on cerebral activity than definite physical or tangible discouragement, but is still effective. By the Nazi example, it is meant that by questioning motivations for crime, for hatred, and for violence, perhaps some sense can be made of it, and the answers to those questions may stimulate alternatives to crime for past and would-be offenders. This technique is sometimes slow to show results, but the results prove to be long lasting. This is the basis on which the Jewish Anti-Defamation League was founded and has thrived for the better part of 50 years, exposing the dangers of racism and intolerance, and encouraging those without perspectives of the past to enlighten themselves on subjects such as the Holocaust and the plight of European Jews during World War II.

Having touched on the tangible cost and cognitive and emotional damage that can occur from victimization, one should examine some positives to unfortunate outcomes that management may use to their advantage. By this, it is suggested that management not let an occurrence of crime transpire and a victim suffer in vain, but rather that future crimes can be prevented though the examination of past crimes and victimization. From victimization, one can know better what preventive measures are needed to reduce the risk of reoccurrence. Certainly one can forecast the effectiveness of a given security measure based on a crime that has yet to occur on the property by comparison to that of other properties, but if it has occurred before, one should take that opportunity to quantify the risk factor as well as the force of the threat. Chess players perform such calculations mentally before deciding on a move by inventorying the remaining pieces on the board, what they can do, and ultimately how their presence and potential will impact considered plans (Maguire, Morgan, and Reiner, 1997).

In addition to types of crimes prevented, research into victim characteristics can provide information on the types of people and social groups that are affected disproportionately. As an added benefit to the study of past victimization, the area of criminal infiltration and criminal acts can be determined. Still another way in which past victimization can be beneficial is that management can deal with problem areas as they are presented through evidence of past victimization, and essentially use those occurrences as something of a timetable for confronting those issues, as if on a first-come, first-serve basis. As victimization occurs and becomes prevalent in a community, it is no doubt brought to the forefront of that community's consciousness, which could inspire immediate interest in prevention or at the very least lead to acceptance of prevention-minded concepts.

CRIME PREVENTION THROUGH ENVIRONMENTAL DESIGN (CPTED)

The crime prevention concepts and techniques discussed thus far can be considered singularly dynamic, a fact that befittingly complements the fluid crime analysis and prevention process with its flexibility. However, one would be remiss in omitting a discussion on holistic philosophies of crime prevention, especially if they can be of help in rationalizing some of the ideas touched on earlier and ultimately lead to an improved property.

The most prominent school of thought and one that is featured in this volume is Crime Prevention Through Environmental Design (CPTED), which is to crime prevention what jujitsu is to martial arts. That is to say that CPTED efficiently utilizes what the given environment has to offer the situation as a resource. Furthermore, CPTED concepts enhance a sense of territoriality within the community or property, which enables and encourages behavioral observation and communication with one another and to would-be offenders that the community at-large is conscious of what goes on in its area and cares about what happens within it.

Three hallmark characteristics of CPTED include natural access control, natural surveillance, and territorial reinforcement. Community policing, when utilized in conjunction with current policing strategy, tends to produce better law enforcement strategies and increased citizen participation in the reduction of crime.

Territorial defense guards against property crimes while personal defense combats base crimes such as murder, sexual assault, robbery, and aggravated assault. As the community tightens, local police can move more freely about the area conducting foot patrols and feel more invited to produce results in crime reduction through interaction with the community. Long-term desired effects would also include an upgrade in area appearance and surroundings, which in addition to being driven by a renewed sense of pride may be furthered by stricter building codes and abatement laws.

CPTED programs have proven to work in dilapidated areas under various names and with the successful cooperation of involved residents. In such CPTED revitalized areas, storefront police substations can often be found, which act as deterrents to crime and as reassurance to residents that the police are actively involved by being there with them. Essentially, CPTED strives to foster a collective relationship within the community and to local law enforcement sharing a common goal of creating and restructuring an atmosphere free of crime and the mayhem it brings.

Some general sub-concepts within CPTED would include improving external lighting, reducing opportunities for offender concealment, reducing unassigned open spaces (to manipulate perception to read that someone is responsible for all space and that no pure common area exists for ambiguity leading to a crime), locating outdoor activities within sight of windows, designating walkways, and increasing pedestrian activity. With these techniques and others, CPTED works to maximize the effectiveness of environmental barriers and architectural designs to harden or shield a property from crime and the threat of crime. A long-term goal of CPTED produces behavioral change through the reinforcement of the defense against crime and by forcing the offender to weigh his or her options rationally and ideally against following through with the crime. As touched on in Chapter 4, criminals base their decisions of committing crimes on answers to questions such as:

+ How easy will it be to enter the area?
+ How visible, attractive, or vulnerable do targets appear?
+ What are the chances of being seen?
+ If seen, will the people in the area do something, anything about it?
+ What escape routes exist?

APPLICATION

Back in his office, having assessed the situation as a whole and having reflected on what he has learned about crime analysis and crime prevention, our manager settles down with the list he compiled earlier detailing the security shortcomings of the property and with his coded listing of crimes committed on the property over the past five years. He sits for a time alone with his thoughts until gradually ideas pour forth from his consciousness as concepts he has familiarized himself begin to connect with the problems he is facing. Beginning with the parking garage, he confronts the lapses in security and matches solutions to each.

Parking Garage

Problem: Theft from cars
Solution: Install wire mesh from the top of the four-foot walls to the ceiling. This bars quick access from the grassy area outside the garage while maintaining visibility—thereby avoiding other problems.

Problem: Traffic congestion
Solution: Redirect traffic into one-way flow by closing off multiple exits/entrances. There will be only one way in or out in order to force cars to follow certain patterns that block various escape routes and prevent dangerous crossovers by traffic traveling in different directions.

Problem: Poor surveillance on third level
Solution: Direct traffic toward either one up ramp or one down ramp between the second and third floors. Thereby, all traffic exiting the garage from the second level must pass through the third, creating a deterrent.

Problem: Violent crimes (robbery and rape) in stairwells
Solution: Remove cement stair enclosures and replace with glass walls, increasing visibility and allowing light from other parts of the garage to filter into otherwise darker spaces.

Problem: Auto theft
Solution: Install card-reading access gates at entrances and exits and issue building parking stickers. Post signs reading, "Any car not marked with temporary access tags or permanent tenant tags will be

towed at vehicle owner's expense." Follow through on towing to the extent that it does not hurt tenants and their employees.

Problem: Poor natural surveillance from parking garage to building front entrance
Solution: Cut down the shrubs to a height not to exceed three feet and remove trees that impede visibility.

Problem: Improve visibility/surveillance
Solution: Move smoker's area from the side of the building to a spot adjacent to the main building entrance, which will enable smokers to see and be seen from parking garage.

Problem: Poor visibility
Solution: Install lighting, especially on the second level, which is devoid of the natural light dispensed to the more open ground and third levels.

Problem: Violent crimes/emotional well-being
Solution: Upon request, provide employees and clients with escorts to their vehicles.

Visualizing an improved environment and satisfied with his preliminary changes to the way the parking garage will operate and appear, our manager turns his attention to the security of the building property.

Building

Problem: Unauthorized access
Solution: Close off the side entrance to all unauthorized personnel; establish a security checkpoint at the main entrance to check issued ID badges for employees; and monitor sign-in registers for visitors who have obtained approval from the hosting tenant.

Problem: General security issues
Solution: Require the maintenance staff to make hourly inspections of the building; mandate that maintenance closets and electrical rooms be made off limits to all unauthorized personnel and be locked at all times; conduct quarterly crime prevention meetings to be

attended by management and tenant representatives that are sponsored by the local law enforcement; and relocate the pay phones from the parking garage to a location inside the building and nearer to the lobby.

Problem: Personal security
Solution: Seek out martial arts instructor; offer discounted building space and subsidize self-defense classes for building tenants and employees who are interested in learning martial arts and general self-defense.

Problem: Improve the privacy of the law firm on the top floor
Solution: Lock the staircase doors to the top floor (permitting exit only through the stairs from the top floor); install elevator regulation device to allow access to top floor only with a special key issuable only to law firm, security, and maintenance staff.

Though our manager has set forth in motion a formidable security and crime prevention program, it will be his job to monitor the results of his efforts. If they are found to be satisfactory, he will look to improve on the efficiency of those measures, and if they have proven to be total failures, he will re-tool his program with stiffer measures. This part of the job is sometimes overlooked because many consider the job finished and behind them, but really the task is just beginning. One does not purchase stocks and watch them succeed or fail; one capitalizes on what is making them money, doubles down on the winning investments, and cuts their losses on poor performers. Perhaps this more so than any other aspect of the process is the most dynamic for it entails timely action and assertiveness at critical junctures of the operation. In short, what management does after the crime prevention program is implemented will show their level of commitment.

8

Concerns for Specific Properties

Throughout this text, crime analysis has been presented with emphasis on specific properties. In keeping with that line of thought, this chapter focuses on the concerns and potential crime prevention solutions for different types of properties. This review of properties is not intended to be all-encompassing, as such an undertaking would be wholly unrealistic because properties continue to diversify and are each unique when the influence of surrounding areas and neighboring properties are considered in the crime prevention. What is offered is a sampling of properties universal to most communities and the concerns they share with similar properties and other property types. What will become evident is that some crime prevention measures can be applied across numerous properties with varying degrees of success, while other measures will be ineffective or cost prohibitive for other properties. Specifically, the property's discussed include office buildings; schools; lodging facilities (hotels and motels); bars and nightclubs; restaurants; stand-alone retail stores; parking facilities; multifamily housing (apartment complexes and apartment buildings); banks and automated teller machines (ATMs); malls and shopping centers; and convenience stores. Finally, a separate discussion entails the concerns of real estate developers, including architects, initial buyers, real estate associations, and the concerns of insurance companies, which assume a portion of the liability risk.

PARKING LOTS

In the asphalt jungles of America, one of the most common properties one will use is the parking facility as they are attached to most other properties discussed in this chapter, and may also be independent entities serving a number of properties. Because parking facilities are found in all communities, are used extensively, and by their very nature contain the means of rapid transportation, they can be the sites of many types of criminal activity. When managed appropriately with crime analysis and prevention considered, parking facilities are secure places for consumers.

Parking facilities are not standardized, and when constructed, are adapted to the needs of the properties, businesses, and residential districts they serve. Though there are differences among them, generally these facilities can be divided into two broad categories, parking lots and parking garages. Both types of facilities may be either remote or attached to another property or group of properties. This distinction is important, as the criminal opportunities at each will be different, as will the selection and implementation of effective crime prevention measures. What will work for one type will not necessarily work for the other.

Parking lots, which are mostly open, such as urban parking facilities that serve multiple surrounding properties, tend to be safer as crimes can be more easily observed and stopped. More remote lots that are covered or displaced from the property offer less visibility and as such deserve more attention, normally in the form of access control or CCTV. Oddly configured garages may present problems for roving patrols or other visibility concerns and should be dealt with accordingly to minimize that risk. Within closed parking facilities, there may be numerous isolated areas that can serve as hiding places for would-be offenders. This threat can be rendered ineffective by closing off these areas, increasing illumination, or escalating security patrols.

Controlling access to parking facilities may be the best method of controlling crime. Parking facilities can be made safer by equipping them with access gates, parking permits, or security personnel. Access can also be controlled through design features that create flowing traffic patterns and limiting the number of ingress and egress points. Lighting should be even and bright, as crime tends to operate in darkness. Elevators and doors in parking facilities should operate in a timely fashion and not restrict access to those needing to utilize them.

Perhaps the single most important aspect in securing parking facilities is awareness. Crime analysis should be conducted to gather information on what criminal elements are operating, when and where crimes occur, and to help keep abreast of the dynamic and ever-changing nature of criminal activity. It is important to remember that consumers will not use office buildings, stores, or other facilities if they feel that provided parking facilities are not safe.

BANKS AND AUTOMATED TELLER MACHINES (ATMs)

Banks have been robbery targets as long as they have been in existence. With bank management comes specific crime prevention standards, and most bank managers are well versed with these standards. The primary focus here is more on crimes occurring at ATMs, where quick cash is the prime target for criminals rather than at banks themselves.

The necessity to develop and maintain a well-balanced security program is elementary and essential to the protection of ATM banking customers. Crucial to such a program are the balanced applications of effective objective setting, policy development, training, implementation, and system testing. All too often, bank management focuses on the protection of cash and physical assets of the bank, while ignoring their most valuable assets—their customers.

Accordingly, bank managers must establish objectives and design systems in response to threats on their customers utilizing ATM devices.

In general, the U.S. banking industry has recognized the threat that ATM machines pose to the banking public. In effect, customers are often locked out of the safety of the bank lobby and, therefore, totally subjected to the security preparations or lack thereof, dictated by bank management. Additionally, the banking public is lulled into a false sense of security when utilizing ATMs. After all, banks often go out of their way to exude a sense of stability, confidence, and security in the bank lobby. Bank personnel appear attentive; there are often video cameras, electronic devices, telephones, alarms, alert security officers, vaults, safety glass, and two-way windows; and tellers are behind tall counters that instill stately confidence on the part of customers. The message—your money is secure and so are you!

To further illustrate the general banking industry understanding of the dangers posed to ATM customers, the American Banker's Association and the Bank Administration Institute launched a victimization study of ATM-related crime. This study was initiated in response to proposed federal legislation that would mandate nationwide minimum requirements for ATM locations to include such minimum standards as alarm systems, surveillance cameras, secure enclosures, and ATM crime prevention education programs for customers.

The banking industry has known for years that ATM crime is a growing problem. For example, in an article published in a prominent banking industry journal, the following list of recommendations was contributed by industry experts to improve customer safety while utilizing ATM devices:

1. determining the crime risk in the geographical surroundings;
2. locating new ATMs in highly visible areas;
3. providing sufficient lighting at and around the ATMs;
4. educating customers periodically by mailing a notice advising of risks associated with using the ATM and how to avoid these risks;

5. maintaining shrubbery and other environmental features at a height at which they cannot be used for concealment;
6. conducting and documenting periodic security surveys at the ATM;
7. providing a direct-line phone to law enforcement or bank security so that customers can call for assistance around the clock; and
8. educating bank personnel to be responsive and sensitive to customer claims and to communicate such claims immediately to bank security (Marshall and Pylitt, 1987).

ATM crimes have become a nationwide dilemma that customers and bank operators must face. Security deficiencies at banks can play a critical, contributory role in attacks on customers and are of paramount importance when considering vulnerabilities and causation in civil litigation. The ATM was never intended as a replacement for the safety and security of the banking lobby.

STAND-ALONE RETAIL STORES

Stand-alone retail stores are also prime targets for criminals. Retail stores include auto parts stores, jewelry stores, grocery stores, department stores, bookstores, clothing stores, and a host of other merchandise sellers. Convenience stores by definition also fall under this category, but their unique circumstances are looked at in a separate section in this chapter.

Customers in stand-alone retail stores usually come with money and credit cards, both of which are targets. Violent crime is a threat, though customers may find it less likely as these types of properties generally adhere to more conventional atmospheres where nonconforming behavior is tolerated less than in uninhibiting properties such as nightclubs. However, when violent episodes do occur, the reaction from customers may be stronger because it is less expected. Retail stores are susceptible to a wide variety of crimes, but the paramount concern among loss prevention managers remains shoplifting. Shoplifting in stand-alone environments may be considered easier for offenders because they can disappear quickly out into the street, into vehicles, or into surrounding properties as compared to shopping malls, where the offender will likely still be within the confines of the building after the theft. Theft in retail stores is not limited to merchandise. Customers can also be victims of thievery (pick-pocketing and purse-snatching). Management should consider that customers of many retail stores are often women.

Crime before or after store hours may also be a problem for stand-alone retail stores. This includes two types of situations, one where management or staff is inside executing opening or closing procedures such as restocking, reconciliation of cash register drawers, or other preparatory measures; and the other when the property is completely uninhabited. Naturally, if one had to choose between the two situations, the preferred choice would be the latter, when the possibility of store employees being injured or taken hostage is a non-factor. Doubtless, management wishes neither would occur, but merchandise in stores is insured and can be replaced; human life, on the other hand, cannot be replaced.

Crime analysis again is a starting point for prevention. By gathering clues as to the intensity of crime on the property as well as the nature of that crime, management will realize the lengths they will need to go to eradicate the criminal elements from the business equation. In some cases, management will make the determination whether such measures as CCTV are necessary and cost-efficient for the operation. While CCTV may not deter all crimes, it may serve to prosecute offenders who are caught shoplifting. CCTV can help reduce labor requirements, especially in stores that do not enjoy an interior layout where all areas are clearly visible at all times. Management can also make effective use of CCTV by openly declaring that it is being utilized and that shoplifters will be prosecuted. An extreme, yet unmistakably clear example was found in a pawnshop located in a high-crime area, where the following words were posted: "Shoplifting is easy; living through it is hard: Our guard will shoot you graveyard dead."

As with other properties that collect large sums of money, secured safes and timely bank deposits are ways to minimize risk and deflect the possibility of robbery. Cash register and money handling protocol should not be deviated from, and all store policies regarding misappropriation of store inventory should be enforced. Store doors should be locked precisely at the appropriate times, store interiors should be kept as neat as possible, and interior layouts should be free of visual impediments as business and space allow. Finally, the potential deterrence effect of store clerks should be maximized to prevent shortages by external sources. Clear lines of visibility for staff is vital to reduce shoplifting and other crimes, though staff training should be instituted so violence escalation can be avoided when clerks confront shoplifters.

STRIP CENTERS AND SHOPPING MALLS

Malls and shopping centers often confront similar concerns as retail stores on a grander scale as they occupy more space, more people visit, and there is more merchandise. Shopping centers are essentially collections of retail stores and other properties in a large building or group of buildings that share common areas such as parking lots and storage areas. Strip centers with many restaurants, bars, and nightclubs may require more security measures than their retail-only counterparts (Gerson, 1997).

Because many shopping centers benefit financially from high-traffic locations, and open and inviting layouts, management should take full advantage of crime analysis and prevention. Beyond the scale, the shared common areas set shopping centers and malls apart from stand-alone retail stores. Center management is concerned with security of the entire complex, including the parking lot, sidewalks, and other common areas, not simply a store's internal areas. Even though shopping centers conceivably have more targets than stand-alone retail stores, they possess an advantage in that the cost for implementing crime analysis and prevention measures may be shared by all tenants. Despite access control difficulties, the high traffic in parking areas creates an advantage in its inherent deterrence effect.

Shopping malls are also able to share crime prevention costs with all tenants, though they contend with different dynamics altogether as they are closed in and often isolated from neighboring properties. Their large size and non-standard configurations make surveying, patrolling, and securing the property a formidable task. Most major malls employ in-house security personnel for the myriad common areas, multiple entrances, and to serve as customer service and information officers.

Malls attract many people, with understandable increases during traditionally seasonal rushes such as Christmas and summer, when children are out of school and have time to shop, seek entertainment, and congregate with others their own ages. Simply put, many different subcultures are at work during a given day of mall operation, and this sometimes brings about culture clashes, drug activity, and gang presence. As mall loitering policies are difficult to enforce, the criminal element may be difficult to single out; however, security should be aware of these possibilities by watching for truant minors and suspicious persons. CCTV, roving patrols, parking lot panic alarms, and emergency phones are viable options for mall parking areas where there is sufficient need as indicated by the crime analysis. Though other countries use CCTV extensively on city streets and inside stores, malls, and restaurants, Americans may be wary of such a presence inside mall common areas, though proper introduction of the system may prove beneficial and welcome.

As with other properties, crime analysis is invaluable in assessing the concerns management will have to address how, when, and where criminal acts are perpetrated. Certain mall stores may prove to be crime magnets more so than others by the nature of what they sell, what kind of consumer they attract, and by the vulnerability of their merchandise and cash flow. For instance, jewelry stores may be targets because of their merchandise's value and size, while music and clothing stores sell items attractive to kids and that are easily concealable.

Mall and strip center stores are usually equipped with stockrooms and back doors leading to alleyways used for trash pickups, after-hours exit, and deliveries, which pose concern for interior shortages and penetration by outside criminal elements. Management should institute policies, which require that these doors be secured when not in use, and when used, policy should require two people to complete the given task, if possible.

Overall, shopping malls have a different task in considering their security risks and solutions. On one hand, management must contend with predominantly closed parameters, considerable space, multiple entrances, countless store staff and consumers, and equally daunting parking areas, while maintaining an open and inviting atmosphere. Property management must rely on the cooperation of its tenants to prevent chaotic criminal elements from overtaking the property because once negative reputations have taken hold, public perception is slower to change when the criminal element is eradicated.

CONVENIENCE STORES

There is not an area of the country or any neighborhood that does not include at least one convenience store, from the finest neighborhoods to those plagued by numerous violent crimes on a daily basis. Though technically classified as stand-alone retail stores, convenience stores often deal with more challenges than other retailers. Unlike any retail store whose target consumer can be quite specific, convenience stores strive to meet the smaller, universal needs of just about every consumer at some point in time. Predominantly a cash-based business and one that is open late hours, convenience stores face threats daily that range from shoplifting to armed robbery, and all too often, murder.

Common deterrence measures include a central cash register location, CCTV, unimpeded views out of the store, limited signage in windows, proper lighting, drop safes, and of course, proper employee training. Policies and procedures should include:

1. Acknowledging customers upon entrance, which serves as quality customer service and discourages criminal activity by putting a face to the crime.
2. Completing merchandise stocking and trash disposal duties before the night shift begins in order to be in a position to view the store at higher risk times.
3. Locking doors at nightfall and operating via a window service.
4. Keeping emergency numbers accessible.
5. Building rapport with uniform police officers working the area.
6. Posting signs while not obscuring sight lines into and out of the store.
7. Being cognizant of and reporting acts of crime or suspicious activity to police, and recording the same for management purposes.
8. Making frequent bank deposits to reduce the amount of cash in the store.
9. Requesting payment in advance for gasoline to avoid the additional concern of criminals driving off after pumping gas.

BARS AND NIGHTCLUBS

Similar to hotels and motels, bar and nightclubs must contend with the fact that their customers come to the property typically with lowered inhibitions, or with alcohol consumption, their inhibitions will lower over the course of the night. This fact is not detrimental because in our cynical and often jaded society there must come a release from tension and the considerable demands of the modern world. However, where large numbers of people gather for the principal purpose of consuming alcohol and casting their inhibitions to the wind, there is found to be inherent dangers as tempers are more likely to flare compared to more structured environments. Another concern for management operating a predominantly cash-driven business is that the property can become a ripe target for perpetrators to launch a criminal endeavor, be it against the establishment itself or against one or more of the patrons, who infuse cash into the business coffers.

Violence in bars and nightclubs can result from the generally cramped quarters in such properties and the tendencies of patrons to be less than conscientious of other people's personal space and intentions. Many an altercation has begun by an inadvertent misstep into a fellow customer, a certain facial expression, or physical gestures, which are ambiguous in nature or not particularly well thought out in advance in regard to the consequences of how they may be perceived by the recipient. As with hotels and motels, female vulnerability is problematic and perhaps more so with bars and nightclubs where inhibitions are low, alcohol is consumed, and perhaps the standard of equitable, respectful treatment of others is relegated to a lower level.

As with other properties, the area in which the property is located figures into the level of criminal activity. A thorough crime analysis can bring trends and the proliferation of criminal activity to light so that management can then operate from a stance of empowerment rather than bewilderment. Thankfully, a given problematic situation can be improved on and changed for the better. Staff should be trained to spot signs of trouble from outside sources and customers alike, such as customers who have had too much to drink, imminent altercations between patrons, or someone who is demonstrating disturbing behavior.

Though lighting in such establishments is usually low to maintain the appropriate atmosphere, it can be kept at a certain wattage that customers and staff will be seen from many vantage points and, therefore, not be put in a position that they can be ambushed by would-be offenders. Illegal drug consumption can be reduced by frequent checks performed by staff security in possible hiding places such as restrooms, dark corners, stairwells, and behind the building or any such alleyways, alcoves, or parking lots that might lend themselves to clandestine and illegal activity. Also, clear lines of visibility throughout the interior are necessary to help provide the safest atmosphere possible.

If gang rivalries are prevalent in the area, enforcement of dress codes that prohibit apparel known for its gang significance may be considered. Cloakrooms and bag check depots might be a clever idea to address concealed weapon concerns. This policy can be enforceable by checks at the door by staff security, which simultaneously can put a face to the type of behavior exhibited upon entry.

The late hours that bars and nightclubs are typically open can also create problems. At these vulnerable times, precautions can be taken to ensure safety for all by using safes, making periodic money deposits throughout the day and evening to reduce the amount of money likely to entice thieves, and having adequate staff on hand. Another security measure might be to provide customers with escorts to their vehicles at the close of business and to provide information about bus stops and times for departing customers, as well as taxi services to pick up patrons who are less than fit to drive home under their own power and judgment.

RESTAURANTS

Restaurants share several characteristics with bars and nightclubs and retail stores, such as conducting a large part of their operation on a cash basis and containing people for a limited time period. Restaurants are often open late hours, and sometimes operate 24 hours a day and strive to maintain a comfortable, service-oriented atmosphere where customers may not be as security conscious as they otherwise might be. A problem that emerges is that restaurant customers rarely browse as one does in shopping malls. Assuming customers intend to pay, a restaurant can at any given time be assumed to have a building full of targets, not to mention money collected by the restaurant throughout the day.

Since restaurants typically operate with streamlined staffs whose tasks are clearly circumscribed, there are few people on hand to watch over segmented areas of the restaurant or outside in parking areas. Crime prevention matters are that much more difficult because restaurants don't have the inclination to turn the property into a fortress. Unless some thematic configuration provides for CCTV, security officers, or metal detectors, it is unlikely that such measures belong in normal restaurants. However, the nature of the business necessitates that it operates under an aura of calculated risk. Given the circumstances, this certainly puts a premium on crime analysis, site selection, and resourcefulness of management to run a successful and crime-free business.

During off-peak hours, restaurants can physically consolidate the restaurant population by closing off underpopulated sections of the restaurant and seating customers in a single section where patrons can be easily accounted for, also preventing customers from walking out on their bill with relative ease. Bank drops can be made before the night hours, and all subsequent collected monies can be stored in safes and deposited in banks when staff is at its greatest number. As with other businesses whose employees work well beyond the closing hour, management should provide escorts for departing staff to their vehicles or encourage a buddy system where employees leave the inner sanctum in pairs.

For several reasons, including a younger staff, later hours, and more cash transactions, it is more likely that fast food and drive-through restaurants will become targets for robbery as opposed to their sit-down counterparts. Therefore, such establishments should adhere to drive-through-only policies during the night unless stronger measures are taken. It is also imperative to train staff and management to spot warning signs of impending criminal activity, such as suspicious persons driving around the property. Staff should be able to quickly contact the authorities to prevent crimes. Essentially, management and staff must be quietly cognizant of all activity transpiring around them despite the often-trying scenarios of a service business operation.

OFFICE BUILDINGS

Doubtless, much of the details and considerations specific to office buildings have been covered in the fictitious management scenario, but as a refresher, management's considerations in securing office buildings are re-examined. During the past 20 years, an alarming increase in workplace violence has transpired and generated the need for additional security measures to meet the challenge head-on. In taking building security to task, management's paramount interest lies in creating an environment that is both conducive to normal business operations, yet secure enough to deter offenders from selecting the building and its inhabitants as crime targets. As such, security measures must be flexible enough to handle a variety of situations associated with workplace violence, including disgruntled employees, spousal or other relationally influenced interference and altercations, and, of course, random attacks.

Office buildings have large numbers of people interacting within the premises; however, most people on the property either work in the building and are known to others at the site or are there to conduct business and are on site for a limited time. From a crime prevention standpoint, the open and inviting nature of office buildings means that many people have ready access to the property, including an increased number of potential victims, as well as those with the motivation and knowledge to perpetrate crimes.

Depending on the nature of businesses housed within, office building hours may vary and may be accessible only to management and employees after official closing hours. Additionally, businesses whose employees work in shifts can cause heavy traffic patterns in the building common areas and parking facilities at shift changes. These considerations should be recognized as they often lead to confusion and possible security threats. Understandably, the general crime prevention measures taken during normal nine to five business hours, when the building's population is at its peak, must be sufficient to compensate for shift changes, morning traffic into the building, lunchtime traffic, and evening traffic exiting the premises. Other considerations, and possible adaptation of the crime prevention program, may be needed for those employees working after ordinary business hours.

The concerns discussed may be addressed with measures alternative to an influx of security personnel during peak traffic times, and if properly enforced and maintained, can prove to reside closer to the property's needs rather than exercising overkill with excessive labor. Dependent on the results of the crime analysis, a cost-effective crime prevention mix of policy and procedure, physical security hardware, and Crime Prevention Through Environmental Design (CPTED) may be sufficient to alleviate hazards posed by the substantial population of known and unknown persons, and the openness of the facility. For most office buildings, regardless of the level of criminal activity, environmental changes can prove to be the panacea for the reduction of existing criminal elements and fear of crime, as well as the increased quality of life on the premises. CPTED can restrict access to unauthorized areas by way of natural barriers and means such as elevators that are visible from the lobby and that stop on public floors only with receptionists or other personnel stationed at the entrance. Crime deterrence may also come from increased visibility by proper maintenance of outdoor landscaping, the use of glass walls rather than bricks and mortar, and clearly marked restrooms visible from the lobby. In more complex environments not fully conducive to CPTED, CCTV systems may be viable options to increase area visibility. Though the costs of CCTV have dropped dramatically in recent years, the expense must be justified by an actual, not perceived need.

Policies and procedures, implemented appropriately and enforced, serve to enhance the crime prevention program. A written policy of sealing all exterior doors except the main entrance, along with procedures for inspecting these entrances for unauthorized access, is much more cost effective than posting security personnel at each door. Policy, if implemented correctly and enforced, can restrict unauthorized personnel from entering the property or at least keep them at arm's length until management or security personnel can handle the situation and bring closure to the matter. In some extreme cases, such as when the threat is significant or there has been a history of tampering with doors, CCTV or even personnel may be needed to stabilize these entrances. One primary ingress/egress point narrows accessibility to the building so that those persons coming and going from the building can be easily monitored by CCTV, a receptionist or other security personnel, or even by the cost-effective method of having the building's management office in view of the entrance. For office buildings that house vulnerable businesses, are suffering from high crime, or for another reason where an actual human security presence is needed, management should utilize security officers as a middle line of defense, namely at the main entrance of the building or, in larger facilities, at entrances to separate building sectors.

SCHOOLS

One cannot help but notice the alarming rate at which American schools are reporting violence and other criminal acts. As thoughtful and informed people, our apathy regarding this matter is not justifiable if one follows television and print media for any length of time. A week does not seem to pass without reports filtering in about another child arriving at school with a firearm, a knife, or exhibiting violent or threatening behavior. Social scientists have conducted myriad studies to determine the phenomenon's causality. The task at hand, however, is to assess the tangible repercussions of crime on school properties to determine what can be done to minimize, if not eradicate, this troubling epidemic.

On university campuses, where buildings are generally more spread out than on public school grounds and the population is usually much larger and diverse, students and unauthorized persons cannot always be distinguished from one another and may cause interference in campus life. In this less structured environment where extracurricular social activities are the norm and carry on into the night, additional risks are posed, especially when the possible presence of alcohol and illegal drugs is coupled with the inherent stress of academic life as well as social situations indigenous to campus life.

As with many institutions, budget plays an integral role, especially for programs that do not provide immediate and direct financial returns on the investment. Crime prevention funding is paramount in any business, but for facilities whose primary objective is not revenue generation, a crime prevention budget is difficult to acquire. Budget can affect the availability of electronic surveillance equipment and other preventive measures, such as metal detectors and the ability to procure security officers and provide training for school administrators and teachers on how to deal with crime.

Even if funds are made available, schools often lack the organizational constructs needed to effectively coordinate such programs. This is evidenced by the ravenous condition in which many schools in the United States continue to operate. Put simply, schools are not thought of as properties at risk. But like many other properties, there is often a sense of "it can't happen here," but numerous are the examples of schools where dangerous situations have become a reality. Columbine comes to mind. Like properties that have undergone crime analysis, schools can control their own destiny and work to reshape the organizational, cultural, and mechanical direction of their presence and subsequent future. Table 8–1 represents common problems at schools and possible solutions.

While it comes at considerable cost as compared to other measures, CCTV helps to keep an eye on more students than even the most favorable teacher-to-student ratio and works to create a sense of protection for the students and teachers it observes. Beyond cost, for CCTV to be fully effective where children in schools are not easily deterred, it has to be vigilantly monitored and requires additional labor. Along the same lines in dealing with technology, metal detectors, while useful for bringing to light weapons proliferation in school property, are also expensive to install, operate, and maintain, and additionally affect the time it takes to allow students access to the school.

Schools are prime environments for CPTED improvements for several reasons. First, a well-maintained atmosphere is conducive to learning, and second, its cost-effectiveness lends itself to institutions with limited crime prevention funds. Specifically, natural barriers should separate the various outside areas of the school. By locating student outdoor activities (including athletic stadiums and practice fields) and school-related deliveries around student and faculty parking lots, the influx of traffic and constant activity should provide

Table 8–1

Problem	Solution
Fights, miscellaneous	CCTV, faculty observation, and student participation in preventive violence measures such as informing faculty
Vandalism	Adequate lighting near or spotlighting potential targets, sensors attached to glass surfaces, intruder alarms, lost property secured, and equipment properly stored
Theft	Equipment labeled, certain rooms and doors locked, key control, and expensive or sensitive equipment bolted down
Drugs	Periodic locker checks, home drug awareness and detection kits, and vehicle searches
Alcohol	Elimination of off-campus lunches, transparent bookbags, locker checks, and vehicle checks
Weapons	Metal detectors, regulation of excessively loose clothing that can provide weapon concealment opportunities, acceptance of discrete involuntary information, and vehicle searches
Teacher safety	Check in/out charts for teachers that are arriving early or staying late, open doors during class, discrete access to classrooms, and video cameras in classrooms

ample deterrence for parking lot crime. On campuses where students use a number of buildings, traveling among them to reach their next classes, unobstructed pathways and low-cut shrubbery will help to increase visibility, thus creating a deterrence effect. Clearly marking and locating visitor areas within view of the main entrance can control access to the school. Courtyards located in the center of campus are beneficial not only to provide a common meeting area for students and their organizations, but also to provide a pattern for traffic to follow, whereby students pass through this common area in reaching their next class or activity.

Outdoor lighting on the public school campus is not as important after school hours as it is on the university campus, where life and classes continue into the night. However, public school administrators should be mindful of school activities, which may go on after dark, such as athletic events or PTA meetings. For the university, outdoor lighting can be a disturbance for those students who live on campus.

LODGING FACILITIES (HOTELS AND MOTELS)

The origins of premises security case law can be traced to the relationship between innkeepers and their guests. Generally, people may disregard common safeguards normally taken at home when they visit hotels and motels, and even when security consciousness is high, they have little ability to control all aspects of crime prevention measures implemented. Their inability to control all aspects of their personal security is something that management should be aware of, especially those guests who are not accustomed to local cultures and trouble areas. Moreover, guests do not know who is on the property legally, and management should be cognizant that many hotel and motel crimes stem from illegal trespass. Criminals realize that their chances of conviction are lower because guests are usually from out of town and may not have the time to follow through with criminal prosecution.

Female travelers recently used security consciousness as a consideration in naming the best hotel. The vulnerability of female guests cannot be understated, especially for those women who are traveling in unknown cities. Common security features in hotels include peepholes, exterior lighting, deadbolt locks, door chains, direct phone lines to the lobby, and disposable keys. This last measure, key control, may cause great problems when not exercised appropriately as former guests may have access to rooms (Leesfield and Gross-Farina, 1994).

In deflecting thefts of guest's personal belongings, lodging facilities should encourage the use of safes in either the lobby area, or within rooms themselves. Hotels and motels should carefully screen all employees, especially those with access to guest rooms, to minimize the risk of inadvertently permitting the formation of inside criminal operations. Guests should have easy access to their vehicles without undue delays created by poor property layout and environmental factors. Access to the parking lots and buildings should be limited to customers and potential customers, and loitering should not be tolerated. Excessive trespass problems can be remedied by utilizing CPTED programs and such specific measures as CCTV and roving patrols.

MULTIFAMILY HOUSING

Apartment complexes, apartment buildings, condominiums, and townhomes known collectively as multifamily housing share some of the same concerns as lodging facilities, but perhaps to a larger extent. Like hotels and motels, multifamily housing contains people and their property, but for much longer time periods. Apartment dwellers are unaware of safety concerns while in their apartments and are often asleep, when they cannot react to security breaches and take matters into their own hands. Due to lease restrictions, tenants can often do little to enhance their surroundings, especially where security measures are concerned. Along similar lines, tenants, who do not enjoy the benefits of ownership, may feel less than inclined to concern themselves with the well-being of the property's common areas, including drug and gang proliferation. Without a sense of ownership, tenants will likely be less interested in who comprises the apartment's residents. Coupled with the typical trend of relative transience found in apartment environments, there is an absence of community-minded spirit and solidarity. With such facts comes the problem of unauthorized persons on the property, which results in virtually all stranger-initiated crimes committed. Unauthorized persons may be granted access inadvertently by unsuspecting residents, or they may enter forcibly, but with so many people arriving and departing during the given day, unauthorized persons and their activities can be difficult to track. Similar to hotels and motels, former tenants may have access to the property.

Solving the dilemma of unauthorized persons can be dramatically lowered by a strict key control policy and enforced by key inventory, the retooling of older and decrepit locks, the presence of burglar bars, maintained access gates, and encouraged tenant interaction (perhaps by way of property-sponsored get-togethers). Posting "No Trespassing" and "No Soliciting" signs is also important to deter offenders and to assist in the prosecution of repeat trespass offenders. Management can also strengthen security measures based on the results of a thorough crime analysis, specifically the analysis' spatial elements. In addition, management must ensure that routine maintenance is performed on the grounds, especially in areas that are toward the back of a complex or building, or hidden from main thoroughfares and areas where drug use or other clandestine criminal activity has been known to take place. Management should also ensure that trees or other obstacles do not impede tenant's paths, especially from the parking lot to individual apartments. Unsightly or hazardous materials should be cleared immediately after detection.

STADIUMS, ARENAS, AND CONVENTION CENTERS

Inviting large numbers of people at a specific time and place can also be considered a scenario where crime prevention is necessary, and though 24-hour security is not mandatory, there exists a temporal window where the threat of crime is quite intense. Properties that house large numbers of people are such places as stadiums, arenas, convention centers, and concert halls, which can enjoy a capacity between 5,000 and 100,000 people with parking facilities to accommodate that temporary population. Certainly large venues of this nature are not immune to crime, and despite profound human presence, a criminal appeal exists. However, while crime on other properties profiled depends on the isolation given to that property, crime at large venues thrives on a high volume of people to create distractions, confusion, or provide an opportunity in which an offender can blend in with others as a means for evasion and escape.

While many of the same concerns that plague other properties are present in large venues, the high audience/participant capacity can act as an amplifying factor that can transform controllable problems into those that are not so easily stopped. There are problems, however, that may be unique to such locations, such as traffic flow upon entrance to and departure from the property, pedestrian-automobile interaction, and security for entertainers and sports figures performing at the venue. Perhaps this is a challenge that falls under the jurisdiction of architects and civil engineers, but on the property and in practice, it is management's responsibility. For this task, adequate workers equipped with the knowledge of designated proper traffic flow and safety are necessary to prevent collisions and altercations resulting from indiscretions and carelessness. Some of the other relevant problems are not unlike those that occur in bars and nightclubs, as it concerns alcohol and subsequent revelry on the part of patrons. Within large venues, such activity is common in conjunction with events such as sporting events and concerts, and considering the number of people that can be involved, it is not difficult to see how the unruliness of an overstimulated crowd might lead to criminal activity or perhaps be the cause of subsequent altercations upon mass departure. Combating this problem again greatly depends on the human security presence employed to survey the assemblage and its activities and timely intercession or preventive action.

Essentially, management must attempt to level the proverbial playing field, since the ratio of security staff to patrons is never going to be advantageous for management. However, those members of a security staff who are present to undertake the task of providing security should be well versed in property policy and how the enforceability of that policy can help them to do a better job. If needed, CCTV may be considered as a means to cover greater expanses of territory with one eye. Whatever the security measures chosen, they must meet the challenges presented by the enormous areas on these properties, and the often inconsistent and at times difficult behavior of its consumers.

INSURANCE COMPANIES

Insurance companies, like courts of law, are a force outside the consumer-client equation, but nevertheless contribute to the ways and degrees in which crime analysis and prevention are standardized throughout various industries. As the agencies responsible for the lion's share of premises liability payouts and settlements, insurance companies can exert influence and dictate stabilization. With this leverage in mind, insurance companies hold the power to make crime prevention mandatory and set incentives for those subscribers who seize the initiative and institute prevention measures that, in turn, reduce liability. Insurance companies are the only such entity that can provide incentives for crime analysis and prevention. Of course, insurance companies target those industries or businesses that exhibit considerable risk, and the actions requested are that which are appropriate to the quantified risk. Also targeted are properties that have experienced past occurrences of crime victimization, which validates the necessity for crime analysis. Essentially, insurance companies affirm all that is logically correct about crime analysis and prevention, and deliver this message while doing what is best for their business in order to maximize any advantages that exist over their competition.

REAL ESTATE DEVELOPERS, ARCHITECTS, AND ASSOCIATIONS

Before retail stores, malls, strip centers, gas stations, apartment buildings, schools, hotels, and banks are erected, there is simply land. This is where a real estate transaction starts and where crime prevention programs can be implemented in the most cost-effective fashion. Years, perhaps even decades, from the starting point, factors are at work that will one day form the basis for crime in the area. As a real estate concern, developers must be flexible enough to adjust their defensive measures to meet the demands of the time. Wise developers seek all available crime prevention tools and resources, and exhaust all options to maintain their investment's value.

It is always easier to work backward in looking at an area in pinpointing the time when a property or area changed from desirable to periodically problematic to a demilitarized zone, so to speak. The challenging task is to project future problems and to prepare for contingencies that may arise given the gamut of possibilities throughout subsequent years. At this point, the concern lies with real estate owners, developers, and architects. From the standpoint of value, tainted crops produce tainted yielding that are impossible to sell; a planned community promising stable, family-oriented living is worth less when arranged around an urban war zone.

In such situations, an expanded crime analysis will show where the threshold of crime is for the city and in the immediate area for the given time. A crosscheck of that same area of 5 to 10 years prior may show crime growth patterns and thus be an indicator of how the area will be affected for decades to come. Community developers and architects may opt for CPTED tactics even if current trends do not call for it, as this is the time when CPTED can be most efficiently and effectively included in other property considerations. Owners should have the strategies in mind as a selling point to overcome doubts in the buyers' mind. Once completed, a real estate project is more difficult to retool for security purposes. It is much more costly to barricade existing entrances and exits after completion than it is to plan for discrete entrance and exit at inception.

Lastly, associations that deal predominantly with completed projects and concentrate on the maintenance of said properties should concentrate on writing and enforcing deed restrictions designed to prevent the accumulation of criminal opportunities. Associations hire out security patrols, ensure clear and safe streets, enforce neighborhood curfews, and organize volunteer neighborhood watch programs. One can think of community associations as one of the many lines of defense against crime, and thus their responsibility is serious.

9

Liability/Premises Security

Over the past quarter century, one of the chief threats to businesses and individuals alike is the civil lawsuit. Whether frivolous or justified, the mere mention of the word lawsuit creates a heightened state of fear previously enjoyed only by the words "IRS audit." The paramount reason for this is not so much that one's guilt or innocence (civil negligence) is being questioned, but rather the overall hassle one must endure to see a lawsuit through to resolution, be it through an out-of-court settlement or by verdict of a judge or jury.

As befits the severity of most violent criminal occurrences, the average dollar amount of awards is usually quite high, often in the seven-figure range, and excludes legal expenses and court costs incurred in such cases. Time consumed through legal consultations, evidence collection (documents, records, etc.), providing testimony, as well as attorney's fees and court costs are evidence enough to the travail of being embroiled in a legal controversy. A worse case scenario is to pay out large sums of money, waste valuable time, lose the case, and then still owe a court-ordered judgment to the plaintiff. Negative pre-trial publicity alone can produce as much harm to a company's reputation as a verdict against the company, as electronic news organizations and print media are exuberant to mention a lawsuit being filed. However, when there is a finding in favor of the company, the media coverage is usually not as great. Moreover, a negative story may make headlines over a period of days, and after found to be false, retractions are slow in arriving and even then are not accorded the same grandeur as disparaging pre-trial and pre-verdict remarks. It is within these circumstances that one suffers from a lawsuit-abusive society that also accepts the disclosure of its dirty laundry from the most modest small-town newspaper to feature stories by the national press. There is often much talk before a trial commences on whether a fair trial can be maintained with the media onslaught and generally cynical outlook pervasive in many Americans. It is easy to see that lawsuits spell trouble for those unfortunate enough to be thrust into one. Despite the troubles that follow, one should always remember that the very purpose of a lawsuit is to come to terms with truth and justice, ideals that one should vigorously seek out and defend.

The other side of the story is that initiating a lawsuit has become something of a second American pastime. Lawsuits, of which many are begun with honest intentions, can become ugly when human nature is coupled with visions of potential settlements. Some lawsuits start out this way and deviate from purpose, whereas others are corrupted from conception and rooted with bogus facts and malicious intentions as befits the machinations of greed and selfishness. This is not to say that many lawsuits are not grounded in truth and that the pursuit of justice is not the goal, which would certainly be fallacious, but there are certainly a number of lawsuits that exploit the better nature of civil litigation purely for financial gain.

Sage advice would be to avoid lawsuits as best one can, but reality would interject that there are times when it is unavoidable. For large, well-established businesses, lawsuits may mean the end of prosperity, and for small businesses without the financial net and reputational buffering of more seasoned companies, it may mean the eventual demise of the business altogether. Those who have been involved in lawsuits (even as the plaintiff) can attest to the strain placed on the participants over the duration. As witnessed during the past 25 years, this has become increasingly difficult, and the best course of action would be to construct a defense against lawsuits.

Crime on commercial and residential property is ripe ground for lawsuits. Since indirect factors such as reputation can both help and hinder the value and population of the property, it is especially important to be vigilant against the civil liability's looming threat. This chapter examines what exactly a potential defendant may confront should one become legally entangled. As civil litigation is a serious concern for all property managers and is often the impetus for crime analysis and prevention, additional principles of defense are examined generally with particular regard to premises security elements. It should be noted that specific elements of premises security will differ across states and judicial circuits; however, the global axioms discussed in the following sections apply to most jurisdictions.

Regardless of litigation in progress, property managers must be aware of weaknesses in their defense. Defense refers to not only the typical crime prevention measures, such as physical crime countermeasures, security personnel, and policies and procedures, but also the ability to provide evidence of such measures through accurate record keeping and documentation. Obviously, the crime analysis itself is critical evidence for the jury's review and consideration.

Stepping into another's shoes is an effective method of considering one's own vulnerabilities. A thorough analysis of the opposition's (the plaintiff's through their team of attorneys and expert witnesses) strong points should be considered because they often directly translate into the property manager's actual weaknesses. Here, it might be reasonable to ask at what weaknesses the opposition will strike, when the attack will occur, how the attack will be carried out, and in what form. Possibly oversimplifying this issue, if the collective defensive can take away one or more of those factors, it can work toward shifting the advantage from the offense to a more even playing ground, if not back toward the defense. Armed with the type of research and actions suggested in this book, one has a shield with which to guard against litigation. Considering this, should a lawsuit become a reality, it will not wreak the havoc or create the worry that it might have otherwise done. Vigilance in our crime analysis efforts and constancy in adhering to the prevention plans and measures should allow one a sense of emotional well-being.

Management's philosophy should be to prepare in the boardroom to avoid the courtroom. Preparing a successful defensive plan and strategy is largely dependent on what the prosecution (plaintiff) has in store during the litigation process. To know this information, one must know the flaws in one's business operation from a crime attraction standpoint (refer back to Chapter 4 for a detailed discussion of crime attractors). Analysis and prevention take the first steps in doing just that; with litigation prevention, one hypothetically steps outside the organization and attacks crime prevention measures and policies to uncover weaknesses and shortcomings to seal possible breaches that may exist. How is this different from crime prevention? With crime prevention, one concentrates on sealing the inside of our defenses, whereas litigation prevention attempts to penetrate from the outside, to be skeptical rather than optimistic. By being on the outside looking in, litigation prevention does not consider budget as heavily as it is deliberated from the inside. By combining the efforts of both perspectives, one attains a stronger overall security construct and gains a holistic understanding of crime. The individual understands why crime occurs on the property, what can be done about it, and the full extent of its consequences (demonstrated physically by the presence and words of the injured plaintiff).

At this point, the individual would be well served to familiarize him or herself with some terms and concepts that will figure prominently in this premises security litigation discourse. A premises security lawsuit, as defined academically in Chapter 2, is a civil action brought on behalf of a person seeking damages for negligent or inadequate security against the owners and agents (management and security companies) of the property where the injury or loss occurred. In more practical terms, premises security can be defined as the past, current, or future actions, and the measures taken to ensure the safety of tenants, employees, and customers from foreseeable crime on the property. Premises security may even include a reasonable portion of the surrounding area, including walkways, common areas, and even neighboring threats not under our control.

Plenty of premises security cases are settled out of court, which by virtue of settlement should be considered as the plaintiff's victory because the end result benefits the plaintiff and negatively impacts the defendant. Outside of a pre-trial settlement, in a court of law, statistics indicate that plaintiffs win slightly less than half of premises security cases that make it to this, the trial stage. While those inclined toward wagering might consider these competitive odds, most engaged would seem hesitant to gamble company profits.

If lawsuits cannot be prevented, then well-documented evidence of reasonable crime analysis and crime prevention can limit management's liability and, in most instances, positively affect out-of-court settlements or court-awarded damages. That is to say that one's labor in crime analysis and prevention will not go unnoticed or unappreciated in the litigation process. Caution at this point should also be exercised as faulty or careless use of crime prevention measures may in fact cause the injury. For example, liability can be increased with inadequately trained security officers who use excessive force to stop a perpetrator, or worse, an innocent customer. More subtle liability exposures are common, such as the faulty installation of electronic access control gates to a parking facility, neighborhood, or apartment complex. Tenants, employees, and customers tend to rely on security measures that they become aware of while frequenting a facility. When access gates are not maintained and are in a state of disrepair when a crime occurs, the gates themselves may become a liability to property managers if the plaintiff can provide evidence that the perpetrator entered the premises through that entrance.

To prevail in a premises security lawsuit, a plaintiff must demonstrate by a preponderance of the evidence (simply, more likely than not) that the defendant owed a legal duty to the plaintiff, that the duty was breached, and that the breach was the proximate cause of the plaintiff's injuries. These three elements—duty, breach of duty, and proximate cause—will be scrutinized vigorously during the legal process to ensure that each is proven by the plaintiff, or else the defendant property manager will not be held responsible (negligent or grossly negligent) for the plaintiff's injuries. To fully understand these elements, a discussion of each follows, but first the legal concept of reasonableness is considered. Here again, it should be noted that property managers are encouraged to seek counsel to determine the exact rule of law for their jurisdiction.

The term "reasonable" is common throughout the law and may have divergent meanings when applied across myriad legal situations in which individuals may find themselves. Depending on the situation, reasonableness is usually associated with a level of care. As defined by *Black's Law Dictionary*, reasonable care is that degree of care that a person of ordinary prudence would exercise in the same or similar circumstances (Garner, 1999). Reasonableness may refer to those actions or measures that fall within the boundaries of obligation or duty. For example, if a motorist witnesses an accident, and the given situation does not present immediate or possible threats to the individual, it is often found to be reasonable for that person to stop and (a) do what he or she can to negotiate the scenario to a point of safety (this may only involve calling or otherwise gaining the attention of authorities equipped with the necessary means and charged with providing closure to the matter) or (b) provide statements to authorities as to what occurred based on accurate and truthful recounting of the fact. Aptly stated, the actions or inactions of a property manager will be judged during the legal proceedings by the standard of reasonableness. A failure to act in a reasonable manner, as defined, may indicate a level of culpability or indifference, and the property manager may be found to be negligent or grossly negligent. These terms, "negligence" and "gross negligence," also call for some discussion and deliberation.

The plaintiff's goal and the sum of all effort put into premises security lawsuits are to prove negligence on the part of property management. Such a verdict allows for the plaintiff to recover compensatory damages. As defined by *Black's Law Dictionary*, "negligence" is the omission to do something that a reasonable man, guided by those ordinary considerations, which ordinarily regulate human affairs, would do, or the doing of something, which a reasonable and prudent man would not do (Garner, 1999). Simply stated, negligence is the failure to use reasonable care. When applied to property management, negligence is failing to do that which a prudent property manager would have done under the same or similar circumstances or, conversely, doing that which a prudent property manager would not have done under the same or similar circumstances. Negligence can only be established when a judge or jury finds that each of the three elements has been proven by a preponderance of the evidence.

Apart from compensatory damages, the plaintiff may seek or otherwise be awarded punitive damages, which seek to discipline the defendant for his or her lapsed obligation, which in premises security amounts to gross negligence. In continuing the use of *Black's Law Dictionary*, the meaning of "gross negligence" is the intentional failure to perform a manifest duty in reckless disregard of the consequences as affecting the life or property of another (Garner, 1999). This differs from negligence as the latter implies a possibility that simple ignorance is at the root of the cause, whereas gross negligence is committed knowingly and without excuse. Analogous to crime, gross negligence would be the equivalent of aggravated negligence. Having defined reasonableness, negligence, and gross negligence, the actual elements of a premises security lawsuit are defined and discussed.

DUTY (FORSEEABILITY)

Duty is a legal or moral obligation. Of course, the discussion's nature relates to the legalities of property management, and thus, the type of duty under consideration is of the legal sort. *Black's Law Dictionary* defines "duty" as a human action, which is exactly conformable to the laws that require us to obey them or an obligation to conform to legal standard of reasonable conduct in light of apparent risk (Garner, 1999). Generally, property managers have no duty to protect people on their property from third-party interference or criminal occurrences unless the victimization is foreseeable to a person of reasonable prudence. An example might be a property manager of a beachfront hotel to post "swim at your own risk" signs and to accentuate such warnings should inclement weather blow into the area. That manager cannot be expected to prevent an individual from acting contrary to postings or warnings as individuals have free will with which to conduct their lives provided that their actions pose no risk to others or themselves. However, if no effort was made by the property manager to warn against consequences, then that manager may be held accountable to charges of negligence providing that the other lawsuit elements are met.

In premises security litigation, duty is determined by the foreseeability of crime, meaning that duty follows foreseeability along the letter of the law just as obligation follows reason from a more emotional or ethical standpoint in contrast to the former's cognitive path. Foreseeability, similar to the crime analysis approach, refers to the predictability of a criminal occurrence based on:

1. past episodes of the same or related activities on the property;
2. that the property is in a high crime area; or
3. that the facility itself attracts crime.

The first basis for foreseeability (1) is referred to as the prior-similars rule, while some circuit courts also include the predictability of crime based on the totality of the circumstances approach (2 and 3), which include other factors known to contribute to criminality. Examples may help delineate the differences between the two approaches. The first approach of determining whether a crime is foreseeable is stricter and in legalese has been christened as the prior-similars rule. Using the prior-similars rule, a crime is foreseeable if a same or similar incident occurred on the property prior to the incident that gave rise to the lawsuit. This rule, as specifically defined by various courts, is not absolute. In some jurisdictions, for instance, prior crimes in surrounding areas may also be considered in determining the foreseeability of crime on the property. When applying the prior-similars rule, a judge may instruct a jury to consider only crimes with the exact same elements. In other words, if one looks at an apartment complex, a robbery in the parking lot may be considered different from a robbery that occurred when the criminal perpetrator kicked open an apartment door, knocked the resident to the ground, and stole the television set. However, in most jurisdictions, these would be considered similar incidents and can be used to establish foreseeability. Some jurisdictions may take a more liberal approach to the similarity of past crime, such as allowing prior apartment burglaries to help establish the foreseeability of a rape within an apartment unit. In both crimes, the perpetrator must first penetrate the various lines of defense to enter the complex or building itself, then be capable of breaking into the individual apartment unit to commit the crime, be it theft or rape.

The more complex, yet liberal method of determining foreseeability is the totality of the circumstance approach, which considers not only prior, similar crimes, but also the contributory nature of the property and surrounding areas as crime generators or attractors. For example, a convenience store sued by a plaintiff robbed and injured by gang members on the premises may establish foreseeability of the crime despite the fact that no prior violent crimes occurred on the premises. To do this, the plaintiff may provide evidence that convenience stores are prone to robbery more so than other types of businesses, that the amount and type of graffiti on the walls of the convenience store should have warned the store manager of gang activity, that the number of robberies occurring in the surrounding neighborhoods was sufficient to place the manager on notice of criminal activity, and that the unchecked loitering and alcohol consumption on the premises was negligent behavior on the part of management. With this example, it is easily understood why managers with properties in jurisdictions, where the totality of the circumstances approach is the rule of law, should exercise all due caution as factors other than past crime in the foreseeability equation tend to muddy the waters.

Foreseeability, like other legal concepts, is not an exact science and unfortunately has much to do with context and situation. A rule of thumb might be to exercise caution when determining its meaning and that it is better to err on the side of caution rather than that of risk. Better still, property managers should discuss the elements of

foreseeability with counsel for more precise standards in their jurisdiction. Though foreseeability may expand beyond the scope of the
crime analysis advocated in this text, by performing the analysis, one
has at least made some effort to recognize whether or not foreseeability exists.

Once a duty exists based on foreseeability, the next step the
plaintiff must demonstrate is management's breach of that duty. As
the crime analysis indicates what crime prevention measures are
needed on the property, foreseeability analysis and security assessment demonstrate what security measures are needed to provide
adequate protection to the minimum standard of the law.

BREACH OF DUTY

Breach of duty is the failure to provide reasonable security in light
of the known risk. In proving breach of duty, it is almost compul-
sory that the plaintiff utilize the testimony of security or crime prevention experts to establish the fact. Such witnesses hold such an
elevated status as they have demonstrated through experience or
concentrated knowledge a penchant for enlightening the court
with an opinion of the situation. The expert witness's role is that of
a friend of the court, and above all else interjects into the case a
measure of truth, and despite his or her engagement by one side or
the other, is deemed an independent and impartial module to the
main body of the case.

The credibility of the expert witness helps to ensure the impartiality of his or her presence in court. An expert witness cannot, like
any other witness, commit perjury or in any way screen facts pertinent to the case; those that do are not retained as experts for very
long. Their reliability to demonstrate impartiality and, in doing so,
provide opinions that will assist the jury is what keeps them in business, and deviation from those goals will detract from an expert's reputation. Depending on the nature of the case, whether or not there
is much known already or presented as evidence on the subject
crucial to the case, expert witness testimonies can have a great or

minute impact on the case just as their ability to make cogent points concisely and in a manner that suggests unshakable confidence in their sworn statements.

PROXIMATE CAUSE

"Proximate cause," as defined by *Black's Law Dictionary*, is that which, in a natural and continuous sequence, unbroken by any efficient intervening cause, produces injury, and without which the result would not have occurred (Garner, 1999). Succinctly stated, proximate cause refers to one specific element or group of elements that directly contributed to the crime that produced the injurious results. The plaintiff's burden is to show a singular action taken or not taken by management that would have prevented the damage under scrutiny.

An example of proximate cause may be access gates shown to be in disrepair and that the perpetrator likely entered the premises through that entrance. A caveat to this statement is that if the victim, through some act of their own, enabled the crime, then the burden may be partially, if not wholly, lifted from the defendant. This defense is especially common where a perpetrator-victim relationship exists.

The Role of the Plaintiff's Attorney

In order to present a winning case, the plaintiff's attorney must focus on the end result of proximate cause by first establishing foreseeability, thus a duty, and then a breach of that property manager's duty to protect entrants from injuries. Heavily scrutinized is management's knowledge of the incident as well as documentation of any and all actions taken to deter or eradicate the problem from the property. Involved in the effort of management might be the attempts of security service providers to contact management for the purposes of offering their services. In light of a known problem, declining an outsourced provider's assistance may work as a contributory factor in proving negligence.

One strategy that is often employed is for the plaintiff's attorney to investigate other similar properties in the area or under the control of the defendant property manager. The idea at looking at other properties managed by the defendant is based in the legal concept of notice, whereby the defendant property manager may have actual knowledge of criminal activity at his or her other properties. For example, a manager of three hotels in a small city is sued for a crime at one of the hotels where known past crimes have occurred. The plaintiff's attorney, while trying to make the case, may use crime statistics for the other two properties, where numerous violent crimes have occurred, to provide evidence that the defendant knew or should have known about the likelihood of violence on hotel properties.

The plaintiff's attorneys may elect to show a low level of security at the defendant property by looking to industry standards for that type of property, as well as by looking at comparable properties nearby. Dependent on the type of business being sued, the attorney may look at a business district or a residential district to determine what the standard is for the area. In continuing the hotel example, the attorney might look at the crime data for other hotels in the area, as well as have a security assessment of those nearby hotels completed to learn about the common security practices.

The plaintiff's attorney may also interview public police officers, including those who investigated the crime and those who normally patrol the area. Interviews will also be conducted with on-site security officers, management, tenants, and customers to get their assessment of the area and management's response to the incident in question. Former employees of the defendant may also be interviewed, as they may be more forthcoming with information concerning management's actions. When the perpetrator is apprehended and incarcerated, he or she may also be questioned. Extreme caution must be taken when interviewing the perpetrators because they often are in the process of appealing their convictions and will not claim any responsibility for the crime. When a perpetrator is open to speaking candidly with either the plaintiff or defense, one should still be wary of his or her veracity.

Finally, the plaintiff's attorney, through a security expert, will perform a security assessment of the property. If the property is a closed site (such as residential housing) and does not normally allow the general public inside, then the usual course of action is for the expert to coordinate the visit with both the defense and the plaintiff. The security expert will normally visit properties that are accessible by the general public, such as most business establishments, at his or her leisure, but may also return for a more in-depth review of the facility including areas not open to the public. This latter inspection will have to be made in conjunction with the defense; otherwise, the expert will likely be trespassing.

Defending the Lawsuit

Although security measures utilized or declined are at the forefront of the case, essentially the decision-making skills of management are being tried. Management will be judged, but additional scrutiny will come from within management's own industry, as it is the industry's reputation as a whole that is in jeopardy and is taken quite seriously no matter what the field. The knowledge gained during the process of setting up an effective crime analysis and prevention program will prepare the property manager in the event of a lawsuit. Like the care taken in documenting any significant incident on the property for crime analysis purposes, along with the reporting of security breaches and corrections to the crime prevention program, this documentation will serve as evidence for the jury's review and consideration.

Management, along with defense counsel, must evaluate the premises and attempt to determine exactly what occurred for the customer, employee, or tenant to become injured. This should be done right away before evidence is lost, changes have occurred, or other factors may come into play. One can understand the impact of a jury having to visualize a property five years after the crime occurred. To assist in preserving evidence, site diagrams should be made to portray the property layout accurately at the time of the incident. These diagrams may denote positions of existing lighting (including wattage), shrubbery, blind spots, possible hiding areas, unoccupied or abandoned buildings, and other design features that may hinder natural surveillance. Aerial photographs available through the Department of Transportation, city planning agencies, or private firms can be used, as well as building blueprints, to show plans for security equipment that has been installed on the premises.

CONCLUSION

All things considered, the best defense against lawsuits is responsible property management, beginning with a devotion to protecting all inhabitants and satellite visitors. A plaintiff's attorney will find little, if any, ammunition to use against management for a premises security lawsuit if as much time and effort is put into crime prevention and security as was exerted on otherwise maintaining ownership and shareholder value through such avenues as sales, research and development, and customer service. In fact, thoughtful management will not hesitate to include crime analysis prevention as an equal pillar supporting ownership and shareholder value.

The Future

10

Consider the American business climate of the 1950s with its rotary telephones, dark suits, painstakingly typewritten memos, person-to-person dealings, reliance on tangible currency, and segregated workforce. In their heyday, these techniques, attitudes, and philosophies were considered state-of-the-art. Many were comfortable within those times, and invariably there were those who could never fathom the technological advances achieved and time-saving methods implemented in subsequent decades. Nowadays such people who cling to present institutions without at least a curious eye toward the future, and improving their transaction and communication capabilities, are considered shortsighted.

New ideas in business are evident in the speedy and efficient manner in which we communicate with one another, transmit and manipulate information, use standardized and streamlined processes, and raise quotas. The impossible is continually expected. Change is also seen in the globalization of business, the record number of powerful mergers completed in the past decade, and how speculation can drive the markets into a veritable frenzy. With all this in mind, how will these business progressions change aspects such as crime prevention as it has come to be known, and how can one remain an innovator and maintain efficient operations?

Throughout this text, we have endeavored to generate an understanding of crime analysis and prevention techniques and applications, but how will this collective understanding change in decades ahead? In an ideal environment, crime will no longer exist as the epidemic we currently accept, but as human nature is highly erratic, that is not likely to happen. So, in the interest of remaining grounded, a conscious decision should be made to keep constant in our vigilance against crime.

As we witness changes in the business environment, we can only assume that the trend of large mergers will continue. Not since the antitrust laws were enacted during the early 20th Century has such a trend ever been reversed, and in light of current business conditions, there is no outright line of reasoning to suggest that we shall witness similar reversals in corporate consolidation. As industries are pared down to a short list of dominant participants, competition will likely continue to mount, and as the game of corporate chess sharpens, the margin for error will, in turn, narrow to dizzying proportions. Budgets will be subjected to further streamlining, and stumbling blocks such as premises security lawsuits and consumer churn will carry with them graver consequences for corporations.

As it stands presently, surpassing industry benchmarks and standardized profit margins seems the only plausible way for companies to put distance between themselves and their competition. Of course, this tapering of competitive factors, precision spending, and planning may one day unwind into another cycle of openness, wherein the contest between corporations within a given industry may not be so severe. Until that time, however, corporate management, as well as the independent businessperson, must be cautious in his or her every move and decision.

Change is a watchword not only among those in the business community, but also in the lives of the consumer. Fifty years earlier, consumers were considerably less jaded as they were dealing with what must be considered an overall kinder society that maintained its honor and integrity much more effectively than in subsequent decades. As a by-product of the hindsight acquired within the last half of the 20th Century, an acidic sensibility has infiltrated American culture, evidenced by the volume of sarcasm and distrust leveled in its collective sense of humor, apathy toward politics, and outlook on the future. The current consumer tends to be more inclined to skepticism than in perhaps any other era. Reasons for this are myriad, but the fact is that manifested skepticism leads to a greater disposition toward negative responses, especially in matters of consumer choice. To overcome this, business must go further out of its way to make its products and services that much more attractive to prospective consumers.

Specific to property management and crime prevention, this strategy entails making the tenants, those who are commercial or residential, comfortable with their surroundings and safe within its parameters. Consumers demand that the companies they choose to do business with reflect their sincerity in the degree of comfort and service they provide. Today's consumer has demonstrated a willingness to take his or her business elsewhere if the task of procuring a safe atmosphere in which to conduct business is not met. While modern consumers are keenly aware of price and value, they simply will not put their personal safety at risk, and knowing the ferocity of competition within industries, consumers are confident that competitors can match or surpass what the current service provider has offered. Obviously, security and crime prevention may not be the absolute or pivotal factor surrounding the addition of future and retention of current customers, but hypothetically speaking, can management gain customers by performing a crime analysis and installing crime countermeasures? Possibly. Can that same management lose customers by failing to provide a safe environment for its customers? Definitely.

By the same token, establishing an initial crime prevention program and allowing it to become obsolete, as the property and surrounding area change, can be perceived to be as irresponsible as inactivity. Management should strive to keep abreast of the property's security demands as warranted by exterior forces of crime and neighborhood decay. Annual crime analysis will provide the necessary data to discern changes in frequency of crime, the types of crimes committed or attempted, as well as when and where on the property they occur. Management must be mindful of crime displacement from one time slot to another, one type of crime to another, or from one particular area of the property to another; such instances constitute the fact that crime prevention has been effective, yet changes must be made to counter these transferences. If hard security measures have been installed, their effectiveness should be scrutinized. Do the access gates at the entrance and exit of parking facilities work properly and are they actively maintained? Has access truly been checked, or have unauthorized personnel found alternate ways into the facility? Such facts can be verified by physical inspections of the mechanisms implemented and by cross-referencing the crime analysis to determine if and to what degree the statistics support the integrity of those measures utilized. Of course, if current programs and crime prevention measures have proven less than effective, management should either increase efforts in their present direction or pursue new avenues toward correcting persistent problems. Similarly, if aspects of a crime prevention program have proven successful, management may consider reducing resources and achieving some direct, financial return on investment while keeping a clear view to future changes and the possible necessity to increasing funding once again.

APPLICATION

When last seen, our manager was busying himself with the rigors of revamping his outlook on crime and preventing crime on his property. A year has passed, and the property has experienced marked improvements. Occupancy is still stalled at 85 percent, but he cannot expect immediate changes; this downtime gives him additional incentive for the upcoming year to further change the impression others have of his building.

From his original analysis, our manager found that offenders were using the shrubs and trees located on his property as hiding places. Another continual crime source was the outside areas between the garage and the building property, as well as the parking garage. His first project was to institute changes reflecting CPTED ideals, which he found to be inexpensive and generally effective in improving visibility and the property's aesthetic appeal. He asked maintenance staff to trim the landscape to ensure that the foliage is not so overgrown and to affix mirrors in the parking garage and other strategic locations to provide pedestrian and automobile traffic with better visibility.

His next project during the first year involved revisions to the building's policies and procedures. First, he instituted a policy that secondary entrances remain locked at all times except in emergency situations, thus all traffic into the building goes through the main entrance, where visual identification is made. He also issued each building employee an identification badge and parking garage permit. Many building employees commented that the parking permits ensured them parking spots and helped them get to work on time. Visitors are granted temporary passes and are asked to wear them in plain view while in the building. For the parking garage, our manager closed off two entrances, leaving one way into the garage and one way out.

Next, he installed an access gate system in the parking garage to address the auto theft concern and to reduce violent crimes in the garage. Our manager then increased the number of lighting elements on the property, especially in the parking garage, the walkway to it from the building, as well as in other common areas. Policies and procedures and physical hardware are enforced and maintained by a security director and three security officers.

Having made considerable changes indicated by the original crime analysis, our manager plots out the change in crime from last year through this year. (See Table 10–1.)

The most glaring proof in his program's effectiveness is the significant decrease in violent crimes. Crimes such as theft and auto theft are the only crimes that have not decreased substantially. He learns from offense reports that thefts from the building have decreased, but thefts from vehicles are still a problem, as is auto theft. After considering his successes and the persistent issues, he realizes that the parking garage's access gate system allows exit without identification. From his review of the offense reports and personal inspections of the garage, he determines that perpetrators jump the

Table 10–1

	Original	First Year
Murder	1	0
Rape	3	0
Robbery	6	4
Aggravated Assault	8	6
Burglary	21	12
Theft	145	130
Auto Theft	76	41

retaining wall to enter the garage and then simply break into cars to steal valuables from them, or to take the cars themselves. To solve this problem, he purchases an ancillary device for the access gate, which requires that tenants scan their identification badges to raise the access gate and allow egress from the garage. While walking around the parking garage, he remembers visiting an older building some years back whose parking garage's retaining walls were elaborate brick schemes. He found it quite handsome and feels that such an addition to his parking garage would restrict access from those wishing to vault the four-foot concrete retaining wall.

Next, our manager leased space to a martial arts instructor at a reduced rate contingent on the instructor discounting self-defense classes for building employees. Tenants have responded positively to management's security consciousness; in fact, since he brought in the martial arts instructor, 20 percent of her students have been employees from the building. Our manager's next project was to move his management's offices from the sixth floor to the first floor, which grants tenants easier access to him and gives him a perfect view of people entering the building.

Third Year

When we catch up to our manager three years after he committed himself to taking an active interest in the security aspect of his building, he has recently completed his third annual crime analysis and is about to enter a meeting of what he jokingly calls the Security Council, comprising a group of tenant representatives, the building's security director, and himself. The time, energy, and monetary investments made in the property beginning three years prior have blossomed and are showing up in the most recent analysis conducted. A graphic illustration of the changing face of the property's crime clearly shows that he is indeed on the right track. (See Table 10–2.)

As he learns from his crime analysis, crime inside the building has dropped, appreciably attributable to the identification badges, security staff, sealing secondary entrances, and moving his office. He claims a large victory as index crime is down 77 percent when compared to his original analysis, with violent crimes being completely eradicated from the building's interior. Theft of and from vehicles has decreased significantly as a result of the parking garage's improved access control system, increased visibility, the traffic control procedures, and the closing of two entrances. In fact, two separate attacks were prevented as a direct result of the mirrors, which enabled two women to see the offender before an attack could occur.

Temporal analysis indicates a sharp decrease in crime between 8 p.m. and 6 a.m., and he decides it is time to consider alternatives to his four-member security staff. After some research, he decides that an advanced CCTV system could replace two officers and

Table 10–2

	Original	First Year	Third Year
Murder	1	0	0
Rape	3	0	0
Robbery	6	4	2
Aggravated Assault	8	6	3
Burglary	21	12	7
Theft	145	130	32
Auto Theft	76	41	12

provide monitoring of more areas. He installs one CCTV camera outside to monitor the walkway between the building and the parking garage, and two cameras on each floor of the parking garage. The security officer assigned to the main entrance has video screens built into his desk, so he can constantly monitor the system while also inspecting identification badges of employees entering the building. The CCTV system provides visual feedback and handles the work of extra security officers quite nicely, and most importantly, our manager finds that he will save over $60,000 annually from replacing the two security officers and provide better coverage of more areas of the property.

Fifth Year

The next time we find our manager, it has been five years from the time that he completed his first crime analysis. The building is up to 98 percent occupancy and is experiencing an all-time low in criminal and other suspicious activity, made more impressive considering that the neighborhood behind the building and other surrounding areas have undergone increases in criminal activity. (See Table 10–3.)

Once again, our manager meets with the Security Council to consider the most recent crime analysis and possible changes to the crime prevention program. Our manager finds himself pleased with the candor among the tenant representatives and their benign

Table 10–3

	Original	First Year	Third Year	Fifth Year
Murder	1	0	0	0
Rape	3	0	0	0
Robbery	6	4	2	0
Aggravated Assault	8	6	3	0
Burglary	21	12	7	3
Theft	145	130	32	11
Auto Theft	76	41	12	4

demeanors toward him, whereas in previous years relations had been quite icy. The tenants had many encouraging words, least of which was the fact that there were no major issues to declare, and they recommended that the current course of action be maintained. He agrees. The CCTV system has been a raging success in filling the void left by two security officers and surprisingly resilient, requiring nothing more than routine maintenance. While no violent crimes occurred during the fifth year, the CCTV system was used to identify a suspect in a robbery on a nearby property. Our manager took some consolation in that he helped prevent a criminal occurrence on his own property and was able to aid in the apprehension of an offender from a crime on another property.

Despite the recent success of the crime prevention program, our manager continues to pursue analysis and alternative security ideas. The building next door has been operational for two years, and in a friendly conversation with its manager, that manager has queried for advice on how he should go about handling his building's crime prevention program, which has seen more than its share of criminal activity given its short history. Flattered, our manager responded with advice relating to his own experience and knowledge accrued on the subject and even offered to work with the property manager on constructing his program.

Our manager now belongs to several industry associations and is chair of the security committee at his local Chamber of Commerce, and has given several speeches on the subject, as well as advice on many occasions. Still striving for greater consistency and improvement, our manager continues his crime analysis efforts annually and keeps abreast of crime prevention advances to keep his property secure in the most efficient manner.

At the conclusion of a five-year period, which has seen his business subjected to startling changes, our manager is reflective. Five years prior, his building was a frequent target of crime and, as a result, he was sued and his occupancy level fell as tenants moved their firms elsewhere. Faced with a decision that held his business' future in the balance, our manager made a commitment to attack the crime dilemma plaguing his building, and in doing so found himself absorbed in learning about and practicing crime analysis. As progress was made in deterring crime and building occupancy began to increase, he saw that almost every aspect involving the property was indeed encouraged by his first positive steps. Over the ensuing years, our manager found that as crime on his property continued to decrease, his building's working atmosphere continued to brighten. Moreover, our manager found that his work habits regarding crime prevention and property security remained at an elevated level, and he made a point to continue to address the crime scenario with the same conviction as when it was a problem out of control.

Appendix A
Uniform Crime Report Definitions of Index Crime

VIOLENT CRIMES

1. Criminal Homicide
   1a. Criminal Homicide: Murder and non-negligent manslaughter—The willful (non-negligent) killing of one human being by another.
   1b. Criminal Homicide: Manslaughter by Negligence—The killing of another person through gross negligence.
2. Rape—The carnal knowledge of a female forcibly and against her will.
   2a. Rape by force
   2b. Attempts to commit forcible rape
3. Robbery—The taking or attempting to take anything of value from the care, custody, or control of a person or persons by force, threat of force, or violence, or by putting the victim in fear.
   3a. Robbery—Firearm
   3b. Robbery—Knife or other cutting instrument
   3c. Robbery—Other dangerous weapon
   3d. Robbery—Strong-arm (hands, fists, feet, etc.)

4. Aggravated Assault—An unlawful attack by one person on another for the purpose of inflicting severe or aggravated bodily injury. This type of assault is usually accompanied by the use of a weapon or by means likely to produce death or great bodily harm. (Attempts are included since it is not necessary that an injury result when a gun, knife, or other weapon is used that could and probably would result in serious personal injury if the crime were successfully completed.)

4a. Assault—Firearm

4b. Assault—Knife or cutting instrument

4c. Assault—Other dangerous weapon

4d. Assault—Hands, fists, feet, etc., with aggravated injury

4e. Other Assaults—Simple, not aggravated (counted with assaults, but not the Crime Index)

PROPERTY CRIMES

5. Burglary (breaking or entering)—The unlawful entry of a structure to commit a felony or a theft.

5a. Burglary—Forcible entry

5b. Burglary—Unlawful entry, no force

5c. Burglary—Attempted forcible entry

6. Larceny Theft—The unlawful taking, carrying, leading, or riding away of property from the possession or constructive possession of another.

6a. Larceny Theft—Pocket-picking

6b. Larceny Theft—Purse snatching

6c. Larceny Theft—Shoplifting

6d. Larceny Theft—Thefts from motor vehicles (except theft of motor vehicle parts and accessories)

6e. Larceny Theft—Theft of motor vehicle parts and accessories

6f. Larceny Theft—Theft of bicycles

6g. Larceny Theft—Theft from buildings

6h. Larceny Theft—Theft from coin-operated devices or machines

6i. Larceny Theft—All other larceny, theft not specifically classified

7. Motor Vehicle Theft—The theft or attempted theft of a motor vehicle.

7a. Motor Vehicle Theft—Autos

7b. Motor Vehicle Theft—Trucks and buses

7c. Motor Vehicle Theft—Other vehicles

8. Arson—Any willful or malicious burning or attempt to burn, with or without intent to defraud, a house, public building, motor vehicle or aircraft, or personal property of another.

8a–g. Arson—Structural

8h–i. Arson—Mobile

8j.   Arson—Other

Appendix B
Uniform Crime Report Coding System

PART I—OFFENSES

1. Murder
2. Rape
3. Robbery
4. Aggravated Assault
5. Burglary
6. Theft
7. Motor Vehicle Theft
8. Arson

PART II—OFFENSES

9. Other Assaults
10. Forgery and Counterfeiting
11. Fraud
12. Embezzlement
13. Stolen Property—Buying, receiving, possessing
14. Vandalism
15. Weapons—Carrying, possessing, etc.

16. Prostitution and Commercialized Vice
17. Sex Offenses
18. Drug Abuse Violations
19. Gambling
20. Offenses Against the Family and Children
21. Driving Under the Influence
22. Liquor Laws
23. Drunkenness
24. Disorderly Conduct
25. Vagrancy
26. All other offenses
27. Suspicion
28. Curfew and Loitering Laws (persons under 18)
29. Runaways (persons under 18)

Appendix C
Common Crime Analysis Formulas

VIOLENT CRIME RATE (VCR) FORMULA

To calculate the Violent Crime Rate (VCR) for a property:

VCR = (Total Violent Crime/Average Daily Traffic) × 1,000

To calculate the VCR for other areas, including cities, counties, states, or the nation:

VCR = (Total Violent Crime/Population) × 1,000

PROPERTY CRIME RATE (PCR) FORMULA

To calculate the Property Crime Rate (PCR) for a property:

PCR = (Total Property Crime/Number of Targets) × 1,000

Note that with property crime, the targets are different. Property crime targets are property, not people, thus the denominator is the number of property crime targets rather than the number of people.

References List

Barnes, G. C. 1995. Defining and optimizing displacement, in *Crime and place*, J. E. Eck and D. Weisburd, eds. Monsey, NY: Criminal Justice Press and Police Executive Research Forum.

Barr, R., and K. Pease. 1990. Crime placement, displacement and deflection, in *Crime and justice: a review of research*, vol. 12, M. Tonry and N. Morris, eds. Chicago: University of Chicago Press.

Blake, W. F., and W. F. Bradley. 1999. *Premises security: a guide for security professionals and attorneys*. Boston: Butterworth–Heinemann.

Bouloukos, A. C., and G. Farrell. 1997. On the displacement of repeat victimization, in *Rational choice and situational crime prevention: theoretical foundations*, G. Newman, R. V. Clark, and S. G. Shoham, eds. Hanover, NH: Dartmouth University Press.

Bureau of Justice Assistance. 1997. *Crime prevention and community policing: a vital partnership* (NCJ 166819). Washington, DC: U.S. Department of Justice, Office of Justice Programs, Bureau of Justice Assistance.

Clarke, R. V. 1997. *Situational crime prevention: successful case studies*. Albany, NY: Harrow and Heston.

Clarke, R. V., and M. Felson. 1993. *Advances in criminological theory: routine activity and rational choice*, vol. 5. New Brunswick, NJ: Transactions Publishers.

Cornish, D., and R. V. Clarke. 1987. Understanding crime displacement: an application of rational choice theory. *Criminology* 25:933–947.

Crowe, T. D. 1991. *Crime prevention through environmental design*. Boston: Butterworth–Heinemann.

DeFrances, C. J., S. K. Smith, and P. A. Langan. 1995. Civil justice survey of state courts, 1992: civil jury cases and verdicts in large counties, 1992 (NCJ 154346). Washington, DC: U.S. Department of Justice, Office of Justice Programs, Bureau of Justice Statistics.

DeFrances, C. J., and M. F. X. Litras. 1996. Civil justice survey of state courts, 1996: civil jury cases and verdicts in large counties, 1996 (NCJ 173426). Washington, DC: U.S. Department of Justice, Office of Justice Programs, Bureau of Justice Statistics.

Doyle, A. C. 1986. *Sherlock Holmes: the complete novels and stories*, vol. I. New York: Bantam Books.

Eck, J. E. 1997. Preventing crime: what works, what doesn't, what's promising: a report to the United States Congress, preventing crime at places. Washington, DC: U.S. Department of Justice, Office of Justice Programs, National Institute of Justice.

Eck, J. E. 1993. The threat of crime displacement. *Criminal Justice Abstracts* 25:527–46.

Eck, J. E., and D. Weisburd. 1995. *Crime and place*. Monsey, NY: Criminal Justice Press (Police Executive Research Forum).

Eisland, G. A. 1990. Attacks in parking lots. *Trial, Association of Trial Lawyers of America* (September).

Federal Bureau of Investigation (FBI). 1966. *VCR handbook*. Washington, DC: U.S. Department of Justice.

Felson, M., and R. V. Clarke. 1997. *Business and crime prevention*. Monsey, NY: Criminal Justice Press (Police Executive Research Forum).

Flanagan, T. J., and D. R. Longmire. 1996. *Americans view crime and justice: a national public opinion survey*. Thousand Oaks, CA: Sage Publications.

Garner, B. A. 1999. *Black's law dictionary*. Eagan, MN: West Group.

Gerson, P. M. 1997. An ounce of prevention. *Trial, Association of Trial Lawyers of America* (August).

Gordon, C. L. 1994. A safe room at the inn: liability for inadequate security. *Trial, Association of Trial Lawyers of America* (October).

Gordon, C. L., and W. Brill. 1996. The expanding role of crime prevention through environmental design in premises liability (NIJ Research in Brief). Washington, DC: U.S. Department of Justice, Office of Justice Programs, Bureau of Justice Assistance.

Henry, S., and W. Einstadter. 1998. *The criminology theory reader*. New York and London: New York University Press.

International Foundation for Protection Officers. 1992. *Protection officer training manual*. Boston: Butterworth–Heinemann.

Kaminsky, A. 1995. *A complete guide to premises security litigation*. Chicago, IL: American Bar Association.

Leesfield, I. H., and S. Gross-Farina. 1994. Innkeeper liability for sexual assaults. *Trial, Association of Trial Lawyers of America* (October).

Lockwood, D. 1997. Violence among middle school and high school students: analysis and implications for prevention (NIJ Research in Brief). Washington, DC: U.S. Department of Justice, Office of Justice Programs, National Institute of Justice.

Maguire, M., R. Morgan, and R. Reiner. 1997. *The Oxford handbook of criminology*. New York: Oxford University Press.

Marshall, K., and B. Pylitt. 1987. ATM crime and bank liability. *Bankers Magazine*.

Messner, S. F., and R. Rosenfeld. 1994. *Crime and the American dream*. Belmont, CA: Wadsworth Publishing.

Moore, M. D., and W. H. Bieck. 1995. Case analysis: establishing foreseeability of crime; actual notice of prior criminal incidents; constructive notice of crime risk, Texas premises liability: inadequate or negligent security. Eau Claire, WI: Professional Education Systems, Inc.

National Crime Prevention Institute. 1986. *Understanding crime prevention*. Boston: Butterworth–Heinemann.

Newman, G., R. V. Clarke, and S. G. Shoham. 1997. *Rational choice and situational crime prevention*. Brookfield, VT: Ashgate Publishing.

O'Brien, R. M. 1985. *Crime and victimization data*: Beverly Hills, CA: Sage Publications.

Sherman, L. W. 1997. Preventing crime: what works, what doesn't, what's promising: a report to the United States Congress, communities and crime prevention. Washington, DC: U.S. Department of Justice, Office of Justice Programs, National Institute of Justice.

Smith, M. S. 1996. Crime prevention through environmental design in parking facilitites (NIJ Research in Brief). Washington, DC: U.S. Department of Justice, Office of Justice Programs, Bureau of Justice Assistance.

Souryal, S. S. 1998. Telephone interview. Criminal Justice Center, Sam Houston State University, May 20, 1998, Huntsville, TX.

Taylor, R. B., and A. V. Harrell. 1996. Physical environment and crime (NIJ Research Report). Washington, DC: U.S. Department of Justice, Office of Justice Programs, Bureau of Justice Assistance.

Texas Department of Public Safety (DPS). 1994. *Crime in Texas*. Austin, TX: Crime Records Service.

Vellani, K. H. 1999. Crime stoppers. *Journal of Property Management, Institute of Real Estate Management*.

Vellani, K. H. 1998. Management ideas for preventing crime: an analysis of liability, site-specific crime prevention, crime prevention through environmental design, and violence escalation. Master's thesis, Sam Houston State University.

Vellani, K. H. 2000. Security + service = satisfaction: the perks of private security. *Journal of Property Management, Institute of Real Estate Management.*

Index

About the Authors

KARIM H. VELLANI, CPO

Karim H. Vellani is President of Threat Analysis Group (www. threatanalysis.com), an international consulting firm specializing in crime analysis, crime prevention, risk management, and security program design. He holds a master's degree from Sam Houston State University in Criminal Justice Management. Besides various law enforcement and security firearm certifications, Mr. Vellani is also a Board-Certified Protection Officer and a member of the International Association of Crime Analysts and the American Society for Industrial Security. He can be reached at the Threat Analysis Group at (281) 494-1515 or e-mailed at kv@threatanalysis.com.

JOEL D. NAHOUN

Joel D. Nahoun is a Houston-based writer who earned his B.A. in English from the University of Houston. In addition to his technical writing projects, he is currently completing work on a novel.